The **NON-OBVIOUS
GUIDE TO**

Event
Planning

(For Kick-Ass Gatherings
That Inspire People)

By **ANDREA DRIESSEN**

IDEAPRESS
PUBLISHING

IDEAPRESS
PUBLISHING

Published in the United States by Ideapress Publishing.

IDEAPRESS PUBLISHING | WWW.IDEAPRESSPUBLISHING.COM

All trademarks are the property of their respective companies.

COVER DESIGN BY JOCELYN MANDRYK

Cataloging-in-Publication Data is on file with the Library of Congress.
ISBN: 978-1940858616

PROUDLY PRINTED IN THE USA BY SELBY MARKETING

SPECIAL SALES

Ideapress Books are available at a special discount for bulk purchases for sales promotions and premiums, or for use in corporate training programs. Special editions, including personalized covers, a custom foreword, corporate imprints and bonus content are also available.

Non-Obvious® is a registered trademark of the Influential Marketing Group.

DEDICATION

Gratitude times two: To Mom and Dad.
One, for teaching me, early on, the
importance of looking up words in
the dictionary. And two, for showing
me what full-on engagement with life
looks like until the very end of it.

Read this book for
time-saving ideas
on how to create
captivating events that
help inspire people.
Learn unconventional
strategies to select
speakers, manage
logistics, set a content
road map, as well as
plan and execute
rave-worthy events
of all types.

Contents /

Is This Guide for You?

If you picked up this book, you are not a dummy.

Many business guides treat you like an idiot. Some even say so on the cover. This is not one of those books.

All Non-Obvious Guides focus on sharing advice that you haven't heard before. In this guide, you will learn all about what it takes to create and manage an event that delivers impact.

Everything about Andrea, from her title (Chief Boredom Buster!) to the way she approaches events is non-obvious. So, she is the perfect person to show you what it really takes to plan events that people will remember, and that will also change how they act afterwards.

I have already been lucky enough to hear some of Andrea's insights over coffee, and I can't wait for you to get a taste of the same experience by reading this guide!

Rohit Bhargava
Founder, *Non-Obvious Guides*

How to Read This Book

Throughout this book you will find links to helpful guides and resources online.

DOWNLOAD LINK:
www.nonobvious.com/guides/eventplanning/resources

You will also see the following symbols referenced in the book, and they refer to content that will further your learning.

FOLLOW THE ICONS:

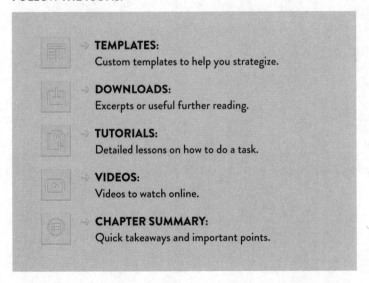

TEMPLATES:
Custom templates to help you strategize.

DOWNLOADS:
Excerpts or useful further reading.

TUTORIALS:
Detailed lessons on how to do a task.

VIDEOS:
Videos to watch online.

CHAPTER SUMMARY:
Quick takeaways and important points.

A sampling of what you'll learn in this book...

→ Do I even need an event to achieve my goal?

→ How can my events be more innovative?

→ What if attendees remember nothing? It's highly probable unless you do something different.

→ Everyone has ADD, so what can we do about it?

→ How do I make sure speakers are interesting?

→ How do I manage unrealistic timelines, implausible goals and results-hungry stakeholders?

→ What do TED Talks teach us about events?

→ How can I "think outside the slide?"

Foreword

BY SALLY HOGSHEAD

Hall of Fame® speaker, New York Times
bestselling author and CEO of How to Fascinate®

Here's a secret...

You don't LEARN how to be fascinating.

You UNLEARN boring.

The sad truth is...most events are boring. They're expensive and exhausting, but not extraordinary. Instead of captivating participants, they hold them captive in a windowless hotel banquet room, with a chicken-or-beef menu and mindset.

How can you design an experience that your audience will never forget? How can you surprise and delight even the most jaded audiences with a new message, a fresh perspective, or an unexpected twist?

In this book, Andrea Driessen delivers the answer.

Since we first partnered in 2010, Andrea and I have shared an intense belief: Fascination is the antidote to boring meetings.

The reality is, audiences are distracted. Your event is competing with every other event, and every other shiny object. Why should they spend their dollars and time on your event, versus others?

If we fail to fascinate, if we fail to create moments of intense focus, then we're far less likely to persuade. People will get distracted by the next email, the next vendor, the next event on their calendars. Your success or failure depends upon your ability to earn this focus. When audiences feel fascinated, they're not putting mental energy into finding ways to escape. They're immersed, connected, and in the flow. When this happens... voila! You're a hero.

Over the last decade, Andrea has coached me on the art and science of the fascinating meeting:

→ Face-to-face meetings are fascinating, because as humans, we engage more deeply in person.

→ It's not enough to just check all the boxes if you fail to create an experience.

→ In the coming years, the event planners who win will be those who understand they must raise their stature and earn a place at the table.

Yes, Andrea's approach is untraditional. No question. She pushes us to think differently about what's possible.

She challenges us to reconsider everything about event planning—from speakers and catering, to locations and themes.

Yet fascinating events don't have to be expensive or extravagant. From a modest gathering in a fluorescent-lit conference room, to a wildly extravagant celebration in Iceland, any event can become irresistibly engaging. This book will show you how.

A truly great event is NOT just education or entertainment. It's also NOT just about giving people tools they can use back at the office. The secret of a great meeting: It inspires connections. It gives the participants something to talk about throughout the rest of the conference, so they can engage in meaningful conversations and create relationships.

Events don't have to be just "chicken-or-beef."

Events can change the course of brands, or lives, or the course of history.

When we meet, we can change the world.

But in order to change the world, we have to meet.

Want to know how? Read this book

Introduction

Whether you're a novice, seasoned or one-time ("accidental") event manager, this guide will give you high-level inspiration as well as tested, actionable and original tools from the trenches to help make your events more memorable and your career more vibrant.

I wrote this book because I wholeheartedly believe that the lively exchange of ideas and solutions matters *deeply* in a world of sometimes overwhelming change and disconnection.

Organizing events that put humans face to face so we can innovate and solve problems has never mattered more than it does today.

So much of our lives is now relegated to a virtual realm where there are more emojis than actual emotion, more electronics than empathy and more clicks than true communication and collaboration. But...

When we face the unknown with curiosity, and gather people in safe, non-virtual, supportive, sensory-rich environments, we build a "sum-is-greater-than-the-parts" world that taps into our collective intelligence. We generate environments of deep aliveness in which audiences can gain a greater understanding of themselves, of possibilities and of effective ways forward.

During most of my thirty-year career, I've been steeped in the events industry. Since the start of the new millennium, I've owned what you could call a speakers' bureau. As such, I connect audiences with best-fit presenters to help inspire audiences to higher levels of performance. It's my life's work and I'd continue if I won the lottery (which means I've already won!).

Then, about a dozen years ago, I had an epiphany that's led to a more innovative service set for my clients.

My big a-ha?

While selecting and curating external presenters is a key step in creating a lasting impact on audiences, what about all the *other* elements of events? I realized that my clients needed help ensuring that their events' messages, breakout sessions, networking experiences, the venue—every single component of the event—*worked together* as a more powerful, unboring, energized, integrated *whole* to produce more memorable, actionable experiences.

How can we engage participants at every turn to achieve 1 + 1 = 3 moments of connection and chemistry?

I realized that I could do more for events than just booking the speakers. I needed to dig into the entire event ecosystem to ensure that all my clients' events sizzled from the first moment to the last standing ovation. I committed to developing additional ways to engage participants that go beyond "sages on stages." I rebranded, expanded and No More Boring Meetings was born.

What I know in my bones:

Events are the most powerful medium for moving the dial on what matters most in life.

And the most successful events are not necessarily the most expensive. To ensure success, we must work smarter, more strategically and more deliberately in designing the event experience.

I read voraciously and learn from a range of disciplines beyond the events industry, all of which inform the *non-obvious* content of this guide:

→ What does a developmental molecular biologist have to say about banishing boredom and boosting memory?

→ What shouldn't you do when curating your speaker lineup?

→ What is ecstasis and how can it improve event engagement?

→ What foods enhance our thinking?

→ Which of the approaches and strategies used at TED events can we use to improve our events?

→ Why are most Q&A sessions lazy—and what should we do instead?

Importantly, this book is not meant to just be read. Like any successful event, this book is about gaining fresh insights—and then helping you *do* things differently.

So, I've also included plenty of **Get Real** segments where you can begin to *activate* and *apply* the ideas you read about. After all, if you're not learning, growing and *using* this information, how will your events evolve and grow? How will you become a more influential and strategically minded event organizer?

With that, it's time to dive in.

PART ONE
Strategy

CHAPTER 1

When You Need Events—And When You Don't

Whether it's world leaders assembling at Potsdam to end World War II, the Chicago Cubs taking on the Cleveland Indians to win the World Series, or you, attending that industry association conference where you connected with someone who would change the course of your career...know this:

> *Meetings and events change the world. They change and sometimes shape history. They change us. It's also true that to change the world, we have to meet.*

It's hard to imagine how much of the progress made throughout history could have happened without meeting. Gathering together. Seeing one another face to face. Only then can we build trust and find the common ground to solve important problems, and if we are lucky, we experience collective and sometimes magical moments that advance our understanding of ourselves and our professions.

The Game-Changing Power of Events (Except Events That Suck)

In a world overrun with devices and digitization, social media and fewer opportunities to socialize, face-to-face events have taken an even more important role. They help us return our focus to generating empathy, connection and belonging, which are all crucial if we are to grow, prosper and create meaning for ourselves and our organizations' stakeholders.

So, it's not a stretch to say that the events we plan alter the course of people's lives. That there is nothing short of a nobility, a dignity, to this work.

Day to day, though, we can lose sight of the big-picture importance of events. We can get mired in RFPs and room blocks. Linens and liabilities. Contracts and catering.

We can forget how much "heavy lifting" events can actually achieve. While I do indeed believe that there is a nobility to designing the event experience, I also know that events can (and must!) be better. We can rise above the daily fray and raise the bar on what we can achieve.

By applying the methodologies in this book, particularly from this chapter, you'll produce moments in time that are rave worthy and game changing for all participants regardless of their job description or pay grade.

> You often hear athletes say, "I left it all out there on the field" after important sporting events. Have you ever heard an event attendee say, "I left everything out there on the ballroom?" Probably not.

With that in mind, when we look beyond the obvious for ways to stage events—when we toil and sweat and intentionally apply the principles in this book—we will produce event experiences that set the stage for attendees to become participants who leave it all on the "field" of the event venue.

How? We work purposefully to design each event element in ways that maximize the in-person experience. We move from **Bore to ROAR™**!

1.2   How to Move from Bore to ROAR!™

ROAR is one of my favorite words. Not only does it rhyme with bore; it actively expresses its opposite. So, I have turned it into a highly appropriate acronym: Return On Attendee Relevance, or ROAR.

> *These days, attendees expect—and they have every right to expect—a return on their time and effort.*

And that return must be in the form of content and connections that are relevant to them; a return in the form of experiences that drive results. Why, otherwise, should anyone pay attention and participate?! Produce an event with mostly irrelevant content, and it's no wonder folks find social media, email and the latest cat video so much more enticing.

1.3 Four Questions That Generate More ROAR

Where do we begin to identify the most relevant content for our events? How do we begin to go from bore to ROAR—when time is precious, and life moves fast—to achieve relevance, collaboration, new solutions and even magic at our events?

In my daily consultation work with clients, I ask them the following four questions as early in the planning process as possible (ideally even before they even choose an event venue).

Collectively, these questions discipline your thinking and provide clear, powerful road maps to success. They help you build a message-driven throughline, and they become the driving force of your event's overall vibe and experience.

Question 1 **What do we want the audience to think, feel, do and/or believe as a result of this event?**

Begin with the end in mind in order to clarify the shifts you want your audience to achieve. This question ensures that you get very specific about the outcomes you want your event to generate, and helps you know when you've hit your target.

For example: In talking to clients about inviting external speakers to their events, I often hear them say they want people to be "motivated," or "inspired." Yet these words lack teeth; they lack specifics. I press them for more details: "What do you want them to be motivated to do?" Then we begin to reach the heart of the matter: "Well, we want the back office to see how integral they are in supporting sales in reaching our $2.5 million target, and we want sales to understand they cannot be lone rangers; we are all in this together and must synch up as one."

That simple clarification allows me to tap into a very specific group of speakers whose content and stories all focus on working as "one team," and "never flying solo" (and we can filter out the other presenters who don't fit the bill).

(For more insights on targeting your speaker search and using additional strategy questions to get to the heart of your content goals, see the Content Map in Chapter 5: How to Curate a Kick-Ass Speaker Lineup.)

Question 2 **How will we engage attendees in ways that can only be experienced in a live setting?**

All too often, events fall flat and border on boring because the experience and content could have simply been communicated via email, voicemail, charts or decks.

When our programming consists of predictable, digital detritus, what's actually in it for the in-person attendee? Not much. They can simply stay at their desks, steer clear of the hassle of road and air travel and "get" the event passively. This lack of strategic discipline is all too common, so it's no wonder there's cynicism about how events can achieve important outcomes.

Instead, as we begin considering various elements for events, ask this simple but straightforward question: What are we going to do together that can only be experienced LIVE? The question forces us to design for emotional, memorable, face-to-face, co-created experiences. For compelling moments in time that are unique to each audience, that have never happened before and will never happen again. For moments and even days of actual listening, dialog, trust building, empathy and collaboration.

Said another way, the question becomes: "What will we do, experience and learn at this event that could never be communicated in a slide deck, video, podcast, social media post or webinar?"

Case study: ## THE "THIS-CAN-ONLY-HAPPEN-IN-PERSON" EXPERIENCE

Imagine that leaders from an educational trade association are meeting in Austin, Texas to expand their professional skills. In an obvious event setting, they'd likely meet in a windowless hotel ballroom, and listen to experts discuss various topics pertinent to their work-a-day lives.

But what if they came together non-obviously? What kind of experience would surprise, delight and engage them with a rich, relevant, multi-sensory, this-can-only-happen-in-person event experience?

You could host the educators on an exclusive, behind-the-curtain tour of Austin-based South by Southwest®, a film, interactive media and music conference and festival. Led by a SXSW representative, the interactive, hands-on, kinesthetic experience takes you behind the scenes to observe and learn about processes that the festival implements for innovation, budgeting, communication, programming, diversity, people management, safety and logistics.

Throughout the day, the participants discover that there are more parallels between managing a school district and planning a massive event than one may think. After the tour, participants divide into small groups to discuss how they can apply SXSW's processes in their school districts.

Finally, the groups report back to the entire audience on what they've learned and how they'll use these insights in their organizations when the event is over.

The day ends on a literal high note, with a special live music performance by a local Austin musician—and a lip-synch competition among attendees. Try fitting all of that into a webinar or PowerPoint!

(For more cool ways to engage attendees in live settings, see Chapter 4: Why You Need More Engagement.)

Question 3 **Does the audience already know this fact, content, data or idea?**

You can generate more engagement and set the stage for a richer live experience by adding this bore-to-ROAR question to your quiver. Once you have a draft agenda, run each potential content element through this question.

For example, let's say you're bringing together a group of network marketing professionals for a quarterly event. The potential programming:

1. **Discuss product updates**

2. **Review regulations**

3. Announce the new VP of Marketing

4. Discuss a key economic trend affecting the industry

Viewing all four of these points through the "Does the audience already know this..." lens, you may realize that the attendees are already familiar with all of this content. The product updates? They were announced weeks ago. Regulations are displayed every time they open the CRM tool. That new VP of marketing? She was profiled in last month's newsletter as well as on social media. The economic news is all over the media. To go from bore to ROAR, you'll need to redesign the agenda until you have robust, relevant and fully fresh material they haven't seen.

Question 4 **Imagine that your featured speaker(s) just completed the session(s) and the event is over. All attendees are departing together, on a bus. Ideally, what comments is the bus driver overhearing about their experiences?**

Sometimes, working backwards helps us get crystal clear about we need our events to deliver.

In other words, if you don't bake in an actual, actionable end point into your events, how will you know when you've achieved your goals? If your ultimate goal is not compelling enough to get people into a room together, then maybe you shouldn't be planning an event in the first place.

So, at the end of your event, you may hope that your "bus driver" overhears, "I now see how we can collaborate to raise our net promoter score by the end of the year." Or: "I wish my whole team had been able to experience that mountaineer's story—it reflects the obstacles we face with clients in a very direct way. Being a member of this association is more valuable than I thought. I'm going to invite my whole team next year."

You want to aim for clear and specific outcomes, reflections and conclusions: "Our new employees will be able to recite our new mission, and will have connected with at least three new members of their group by the time the workshop is over." Not vague, like this: "We want our new employees to be happy that they chose to work here."

As you will see in Chapter 5: How to Curate a Kick-Ass Speaker Lineup chapter, these "bus driver's comments" will also help you get clear on the kinds of speakers you're looking for. They will show you what success would sound like so that you can effectively lay the groundwork to achieve all of your goals.

 **GET REAL:**

You may be thinking: whew. Answering these "bore-to-ROAR" questions is hard! Well, you know what's even harder? Being an attendee at an event that's short on relevance, collaboration and tools for problem solving.

So, which of these questions are you going to commit to answering for your next event? By when and of whom are you going to ask them? What question do you think is missing from my list?

 CHAPTER SUMMARY:
THREE THINGS TO REMEMBER

→ The ultimate goal of a kick-ass event is to produce a "this-can-only-happen-in-person" experience.

→ To get there, generate a Return On Attendee Relevance (ROAR™, and the opposite of bore) by asking four key questions early in your planning process.

→ Use these questions to generate a message-driven throughline that will become the driving force of your event's overall vibe and experience.

CHAPTER 2

How We Learn: Why Some Events Work Better Than Others

In the previous chapter, we laid important groundwork for offering relevant (ROAR-ing, in fact!) conference programming so your audiences can activate more positive change in their personal and professional lives.

But what if attendees remember nothing from their event experiences?

It's not as crazy an outcome as it seems. Most events are often overloaded with so much material that learning may be hurt more than it's enhanced.

Consider the last event at which you were an attendee. What do you recall from it? Yeah, I thought so.

Given the amount of time we spend surrounded by computers—at work, at home, during commutes and yes, at events—it's natural to think of ourselves as Pentium chips. We believe we can keep adding data and everything will be automatically saved on the "hard drives" in our heads.

If only.

As digerati in this wildly wired world, we are constantly exposed to information: from our devices, social media, billboards, conversations, even books! But how much of that information actually sticks and can be applied as actionable insight?

While the human brain is indeed powerful, it is not capable of remembering—much less recalling—all we try to cram into it. The events world is particularly vulnerable to this overload.

Yet events can (and must) be rich, powerful environments where we generate new ideas, solve our most pressing problems and enhance productivity.

Our biggest misconception about learning and memory is our assumption that simple exposure to an idea is enough to ensure that we learn something.

But simply coming face to face with new information isn't learning. Learning only happens over time, when we connect new ideas to our own experiences to make them meaningful. When we take new concepts out for a spin. When we interact with ideas and begin to apply them. When we reflect on what we read, hear and experience. When our emotions coalesce with new details to more deeply encode the material in our brains.

2.1 Why Attendees May Remember Nothing

Let's take a closer look at what happens to our minds in meetings, explore how to boost recall and memory, and in the process, the impact of all our events.

As Jeff Hurt of consultancy Velvet Chainsaw explains: "Forgetting is easy. Remembering is hard. The majority of conference education is counterproductive to learning. Lecture, panels of talking heads, debates, keynotes, verbatim note taking, all create the illusion of learning. In reality, the gains attendees thought they had disappear quickly."[1]

Skeptical? Well, consider this: The same brain we bring to events is the same brain that goes to school. Imagine you're in a class and just heard a professor's lecture. What if someone tested your knowledge about it, right there, outside the door? Would you pass? Of course not. You'd have to study what the teacher said. Reflect on it. Talk about it.

> *Typical event programming and standard information-delivery models are built on the false narrative that information can be transmitted and retained through the simple presentation of arguments and facts.*

But listening and taking notes are passive activities, Hurt cautions. Active participation in the learning process helps people retain and apply new information more efficiently. What's the best way to know if people have learned something from an event? When they can summarize it in their own words and correctly explain how they would apply it in their own lives.

2.2 Designing for Real Learning

So, how do you set the stage for people to more effectively process and retain new information? Here are seven easy-to-implement tips to help you produce events designed for active learning and greater retention of content:

Tip 1 **Be a tapas bar, not an all-you-can-eat buffet**

Guests will remember more when you remember that less is more. No matter the length of an event, you must focus on two or three important messages and takeaways. And no more than that, says Hurt. Then design every agenda element around these top takeaways.

Tip 2 **Aim for a higher level**

Event audiences are comprised of a wide variety of skill sets and education levels. So, should you offer content that's suited to beginners or those who are more advanced in their knowledge? Adult education practices teach us that it's best to err on the side of advanced content—to cater to the highest instead of the lowest common denominator because doing so will challenge everyone.

Tip 3 **Insert interaction**

When we interact with new ideas—wrestle with them, and talk to others about them—we improve our awareness and ultimately learn more. As you select speakers, be sure to invite people who are able and willing to facilitate interaction among audience members, instead of only assuming the role of the expert at the front of the room.

DOWNLOAD

Get a list of speakers who deliver exceptionally interactive sessions: www.nomoreboringmeetings.com/interactive-speakers

Further, as adults, we need to know why we are learning something. Give us the why, and we'll be more motivated to pay attention. We want learning based on actual life experiences—scenarios that involve real play, not role play.

We need participatory environments that give us power to shape how we learn in active and engaging ways.

Explore fresh event formats that are heavy on interactivity in Chapter 4: Why You Need More Engagement and Chapter 8: Unconventional Event Formats.

Tip 4 Build in more repetition, reflection and white space

I repeat: Build in more repetition, reflection and white space

Every brain benefits from repetition. But don't just take my word for it. Dr. John Medina, the author of *Brain Rules* and a developmental molecular biologist explains, "The way to make long-term memory more reliable is to incorporate new information gradually and repeat it in timed intervals."[2] Dr. Medina's research led to the creation of a specific, measurable rule: the information you want your people to most remember and apply is best repeated within just two hours of their first exposure to it.

So, it's not overdoing it to revisit 10 A.M. keynote content over lunch, for example. Reinforcing the content the next day or even worse, the next month, means you may as well...forget it!

Coupled with repetition is the need to provide enough time for people to reflect between info-rich segments. You may be thinking, but hey, I don't have much time! My event agendas are PACKED!

Well, it's time to "unpack" them. If you are truly committed to helping participants grow, you need to repeat the information you are hoping to transmit (using different forms of delivery) and build in "white space" in which participants may reflect on what they've learned.

So, when it comes to planning an agenda, we are wise to include content-free break time, as well as revisit and repeat key points throughout the event.

Few event planners are willing to build in enough breaks to make sure that this type of learning occurs. In my case, the clients who do have happier, and smarter, attendees.

For more insights on improving brain power, including what you feed the minds of your delegates, turn to the next chapter, How to Transform Attendees into Participants.

Tip 5 Recognize that the eyes do have it

We process visual imagery much faster and more thoroughly than text. While slide decks with visuals are common, they don't always succeed in enhancing presentations. Additional visual-learning tools include graphic illustration, 3-D conceptual models, videos, charts, infographics and attendees' own drawings and sketches (even when rudimentary), all of which reinforce key concepts in a stickier way than text can. (For additional visual and kinesthetic tools for delivering content without slides, see Chapter 11: How to Produce and Stage Manage an Event Like a Pro.)

Tip 6 **Tap all the senses for deeper retention**

Since we are aiming for participatory, active learning, event planners should make an effort to incorporate as many of the senses as possible into programming to give attendees' brains more ways to access, understand and recall content.

Just as each of our senses serves a purpose for animals looking to survive in the wild, so do they help humans incorporate memories and concepts into the brain for later use.

Consider this model of a multi-sensory event experience in which attendees...

→ See large whiteboards with visual representations of ideas, as well as illustrations with key takeaways from speakers' sessions in real time.

→ Hear fellow participants' comments and questions in a range of interactive segments.

→ Smell the aroma of an essential oil chosen specifically for its capacity to improve mental clarity.

→ Activate the body with periodic movement-based kinesthetic exercises that help boost memory.

→ Feed the body—and the mind—with food chosen for its ability to boost brain power.

→ Tap feet to a closing song that summarizes key points in the form of a memorable tune.

Smell, in particular, is our most evocative sense, and boosts memory directly, without being paired with any other sense. All other senses are processed through a more complex routing system in the brain, but smell bypasses these and goes directly to the amygdala and hippocampus, which manage memory and emotion.

So, if your events don't smell like anything other than a meal, then you're missing a huge opportunity to create positive, memorable experiences for your guests.

Examples of employing scent beyond the aroma of food include judicially chosen essential oils to elicit specific moods (such as rosemary and peppermint for cognitive ability), a campfire to foster feelings of belonging and cohesion or the smell of sugar to elicit more playfulness.

Tip 7 **Give your content more context**

Learning never happens in a vacuum. So, it's crucial to hire presenters who understand the importance of helping participants see how the event material fits into a larger context and guiding them in getting practical insight out of it—during and after sessions. As event organizers, we must insist that presenters have specific strategies for reinforcing key points and offering insight on how the most important concepts can be applied in their work.

When learning something new, audiences don't yet know what they don't know. Well-trained facilitators and "conference weavers" (another term for event hosts who help the audience weave specific content into a larger, coherent objective and theme) help attendees understand what they are supposed to be remembering and how that information fits into the larger picture.

Content hosts and weavers add intention to the audience's educational journey toward self-improvement. They connect the attendees to the event's message and reinforce top-level takeaways. (See Chapter 6: How to Use Panels, Q&A Sessions and Event Hosts for more ideas in this realm.)

Next time we're tempted to use a fire-hose approach to conference education, in a way that overwhelms people with too much content, let's allow attendees' brains do what they do best: generate meaning by tapping into curiosity, creativity and consciousness.

GET REAL:

Retrieve your notes from an event session you attended. Then review key points from this chapter about how learning sticks, and apply at least one of the above seven principles to a session that you experienced so you can see new, more learner-friendly possibilities in its redesign.

 CHAPTER SUMMARY:
THREE THINGS TO REMEMBER

→ Coming face to face with new information is not learning.

→ Active participation helps people retain and apply new information more efficiently.

→ Interactivity, repetition, visual aids and tapping all five senses (sight, sound, touch, taste, and smell) improve learning.

CHAPTER 3

How to Transform Attendees into Participants

Hail all brain researchers! These folks are heroes to the events industry. Their efforts and experiments reveal crucial and fascinating truths about how we learn, how information and memories stick in our minds and how we can design better event environments.

For example, brain science reveals that exercise and movement have significant impacts on our brains' abilities to process and retain information. In short, the more we sit, the more we forget; the more we move, the more we learn.

(Wow—way to go, brain!)

Why Movement Is Crucial

Think about most event experiences, though: they involve sitting. A lot. But science says this is wrong.[3] "Exercise is a terrific way to improve the learner because it turns on the attention system, the motivation system and the memory system...and optimizes the brain's ability to learn as well as helps regulate emotions,"[4] notes Dr. John Ratey, author of *SPARK: The Revolutionary New Science of Exercise and the Brain.*

According to brain researcher, Dr. Medina, whom we met in the previous chapter, exercise boosts brain power in three main ways:

→ It increases blood flow to the brain, bringing it glucose which increases energy and oxygen to soak up the toxic electrons.

→ It strengthens and quickens the connections between neurons.

→ It acts directly on the molecular machinery of the brain itself, increasing neuron creation, survival and resistance to damage and stress.[5]

Don't you wish you'd known this when sitting at a desk, cramming for hours in school?

So, if you're truly committed to turning attendees into participants (so they "leave it all on the ballroom floor," as we discussed in the introduction), you gotta get folks out of their chairs and actively involved.

Here are some non-obvious examples of how to boost movement at your events—well beyond the old standby of golf.

→ Try a simple "walk and talk." Noted in more detail in Chapter 8: Unconventional Event Formats, this experience sends pairs of people in walks around a room, an entire venue or a city block to discuss a pertinent topic.

→ Need to get folks from the ballroom to the bus? At registration, ask everyone to bring an item that represents their home town or their company (but don't explain why). Ask them to bring it to the appointed event session, after which your host leads them in a parade to dinner-bound buses. The highly personal items become conversation pieces, the walk loosens stiff bodies and your attendees become participants in their own memorable parade. Provide hand-held musical instruments and flags to those who didn't bring something from home.

Consider, too, the following five activities that promote movement (and could be provided by a mover-and-shaker-type sponsor to help defray costs):

1. Set up a bank of spin bikes for a straightforward way to burn off energy.

2. Do you really need chairs throughout the entire event? Bring in some exercise (stability) balls, and turn a staid ballroom into a literal ball room. The novelty will spark a different kind of thinking, and the physical movement will keep the mind in motion.

3. Offer a few ping pong tables in the break area for welcomed mental breaks and easy networking.

4. Put modeling clay on the tables in place of centerpieces and suggest that participants Instagram their creations.

5. Stage a laser tag competition in a lounge or on a lawn during your reception.

The same way that effective workouts help us acquire new physical abilities, great events can push us to expand our understanding of our own capabilities.

 ## Timing Matters: Are Your Events Backwards?

Bestselling author and TED speaker Shawn Achor is a top researcher whose work is casting a bright light on event design. In one of his books, *Before Happiness*, he discusses **how to structure gatherings to maximize our brain power.**

At most conferences, presenters begin by making vague comments on a broad topic, then present themes and courses for exploration. The attendees are often divided into smaller groups for deeper education and application. These breakouts often continue until lunchtime (and long after breakfast), with exercises that require heady integration and deep thinking about the topics to which the audience has just recently been exposed. Then, the same keynote/breakout/cram session model is scheduled for the afternoon, ending just before dinner. (Whew— pass the margarita pitcher, please!)

Yet, as Achor's research points out, our brains are least able to handle full-on cognitive tasks hours after we have eaten. He explains how, given traditional meeting agendas, "...the most critical plans and decisions are made when our brain glucose is the most depleted [i.e. right before a meal]. We are doing conferences backward!"[6]

Instead, be sure attendees are doing their most critical thinking *within an hour after breakfast,* or *within an hour after lunch* when the brain's glucose levels are optimized. And, when giving attendees a break between activities, offer them brain-friendly snacks to set everyone up for success.

Hungry for more in this realm? See Chapter 8: Unconventional Event Formats.

3.3 Fostering a Greater Audience Intelligence

One of the most effective ways to help participants learn new ideas and take on new behaviors in an event setting is to help them become so absorbed in an experience that they forget they're even at an event. You want them to become so focused on what they're doing, that distractions fall away and the learning is more like real life than "event life."

The power of immersive learning to me is embodied in the Greek word ecstasis, which means the "act of stepping beyond oneself." In the book *Stealing Fire*, authors Steven Kotler and Jamie Wheal use the term in a more modern sense—in a context that can inspire us in the events world.[7]

For when we reach a state of ecstasis, we have "a powerful connection to a greater intelligence." This is what scientists today call "group flow" or a state of possibility, awareness and activation. That, to me, is the ultimate goal when engaging people in events, and it can only happen when we become deeply immersed in what we are doing.

Those in training and development call this immersive learning—being fully in the learning experience. Practicing. Failing. Deciding. Leading. Operating. Improving.

In these rarified environments, we're fully engaged in the now.

IMMERSIVE LEARNING

One of my clients faced a common challenge: They wanted their teams to learn to "think like customers and owners," and to understand, viscerally, what it feels like to be on the receiving end of mediocre service. They wanted the experience to feel so real that it would stick. So, we didn't rely on outside customer service experts to tell them how to deliver service more effectively, as this was a well-worn route.

Instead, I designed a powerful way for the audience to have a poor customer experience themselves by turning the event experience on its head.

When employees arrived on site, signage was in another language. Attendees were given no agenda, so they had no idea what to expect, at least in the initial hours of the meeting. "Usual" departmental teams were split up. Dessert was served as the first course. You get the idea.

You can see how we intentionally made the familiar unfamiliar. As is the case with an organization's consumers, clients and new employees, uncertainty affects our abilities to engage.

But when we staged an immersive event experience and made it as "day-in-the-life-real" as possible, we helped learners replace role play with real play in ways tied to the organization's actual business objectives and service goals.

After participants realized that they had experienced a setup of sorts, they reported in positively. "Ha! Now I better get what it's like to experience crummy service in the context of our brand. I'll be much more able to empathize with clients in the future." Another said: "When I walked in for breakfast and the ballroom was a mess and not ready, I got angry and confused. Then I was like, 'Oh, so now when my team and I show up for a meeting with a prospect, if we are not 100% dialed in and prepped, I know exactly how that feels.' Smart move, meeting planners!"

3.4 How to Select the Right Food for Your Event

Eating at meetings: what you feed people matters

All this talk of movement and meals has me craving insights on how to feed our bodies what they need to perform at their best.

If we want attendees to focus and function well, we must consume the very best, brain-friendly foods.

Here's what attendees' brains are hungry for, and what they're not:

→ According to writer and wellness expert Jennifer Cohen, the best foods for brain power are dark chocolate (hallelujah!), celery, bee pollen, bone broth, sun flower, chia and pumpkin seeds, beets, spinach, coconut oil, walnuts, maca (a root in the radish family) and turmeric.[8] These can be combined in something as simple as a trail mix, added as seasoning or served as side dishes.

→ When you want people to doze off, serve carbo-hydratezzzzz (muffins, cookies, soda). If you want them to be engaged and alert, pile on the protein: fish and chicken maintain energy (and red meat lowers it). Boost the brain with peanut and almond butter, as well as other low-glycemic snacks and energy bars.

→ Whether you're eating a meal or a snack, avoid white sugar, white (non-wheat) flour, regular rice and too many starches like spuds. And while it is white, yogurt is a superb snack and great source of protein. To satisfy the sweet tooth? Fresh fruit, naturally.

 GET REAL:

Why not take this list of brain-boosting foods to your caterer to see what they can cook up for your breaks? And, next time you're attending an event as a participant, bring some snacks you know your brain craves and take note of how you feel and perform.

In the meantime, my hope is that some entrepreneurially hungry business person-cum-chef will mix up a game-changing snack food that deliciously incorporates many of these brain-friendly ingredients into a super-brain-power nosh for future events.

 CHAPTER SUMMARY:
THREE THINGS TO REMEMBER

→ The more we sit, the more we forget; the more we move, the more we learn.

→ Exercise and movement also heighten attention, motivation and memory.

→ What we eat and when we eat it matter at events, and impact productivity and engagement.

CHAPTER 4

Why You Need More Engagement and How to Get It

You may have heard that the human attention span is nine seconds ("same as a gold fish") or more generously, twenty minutes (about the maximum length of a TED Talk).

In reality, people's attention spans vary by circumstance. Bottom line:

Our attention span is very short, it's shrinking and it's generally much shorter than most event segments, which tend to clock in at two to four *hours*.

We also know that capturing—and *keeping*—the attention of audiences is the holy grail of our events. We know that people who are engaged and attentive are more focused, are more able to learn, and are more likely to have the mental bandwidth and social willingness to collaborate and solve pressing challenges.

What we and our event attendees pay attention to— what gives us all meaning—results in how we spend our hours, our days and our lives. Move over, bitcoin. Attention is our most valuable currency.

But what, really, does it mean to be engaged? What does it look like, and how do we actually *get* there? How can we create content that's *worth* participants' time?

That's where we'll put *our attention* in this chapter.

4.1 Why So Many Business Events Fail

The most successful events are collaborative think tanks ("hive minds") that effectively tackle the organization's participants' top challenges. Participatory event elements teach us that we are all connected, and that we are capable of fostering a collective meeting intelligence. If your event doesn't facilitate multiple ways for people to work *together* to problem solve, everyone may as well stay home.

Said more succinctly:

If participants don't engage and participate in co-creating content that matters to *them*, we have failed as event organizers.

So, how *do* we set the stage for our audiences to be maximumly engaged?

People engage with what matters to them based on their own self-interest. Nothing more and nothing less. You could stage the best event the world has ever seen. But if no one knows, or not enough of the "right" people attend, all your efforts are for naught.

No one registers for an event thinking, "I hope there will be a great deal of information and data." "Let's see if the educational sessions focus on what I already know." "I care most about all the speakers' accomplishments." "I wonder if the networking reception will be the same as last year."

Too many business events fail to deliver impact because they don't approach content development from the audience's point of view.

4.2 **What People Really Want from Events**

→ Collaborative problem solving.

→ Incremental progress toward important milestones.

→ Tools for increased productivity.

→ Connecting with others who will make positive differences in their lives.

→ Co-creating on ideas that matter.

→ Feeling heard.

→ Contributing to crucial initiatives.

→ Being part of a special community.

To illustrate, here's an **example of *failure* to capitalize on opportunities for collaboration and connection:**

Not long ago, I attended a large, global convention. Since this gathering was planned by a team of top meeting planners, you'd think it would exemplify best-in-class design. Nope. The opening keynote speaker, an expert and author on *collaboration* no less, did absolutely nothing in his thirty minutes to bring together the thousands of people in the audience. He just talked at us. On the simplest level, he could have offered, "Turn to your neighbor and share one insight you'd like to gain this week, a challenge you're looking to solve or one person you'd like to meet." *Ba da bing!* A massive hive mind alive with connection, collaboration and activation.

Now an **example of a simple, affordable and powerful way to generate engagement in an event setting:**

At the annual Summer Institute for Intercultural Communication, participants take a deep dive on the topic of diversity and inclusion to heighten their intercultural communication skills. Early in the week, they're all given plain T-shirts and indelible ink markers. Then, they are asked to draw a simple pictogram illustrating how they view their level of intercultural awareness. After a week's worth of workshopping, they're asked to draw another pictogram showing their *new* level of understanding. Then the host facilitates a highly collaborative and interactive conversation about the shifts each person experienced throughout the conference, using their pictograms as tangible (and wearable!) storytelling tools.

 ## How to Engage People Across Generations

In addition to knowing what your attendees want, you gotta know *how* they want it.

Just as we all like a pizza with our favorite toppings, each generation has distinct ways in which they prefer to "get" information. According to Amy Lynch, a generational consultant, keynoter and CEO of Generational Edge, we can still keep the attention of 50+ audiences with a "top-down" approach where you place someone on stage who knows something the audience doesn't, and tell the audience what that something is. Most in the older set accept this "sage-on-the-stage" scenario.[9]

This is not the case with many younger members of your audience.

To connect with Millennials (AKA Gen Y), Gen-X and Gen Z, we must rethink what it means to share information.

No more top down. Instead, aim for interaction between the speaker and the audience—the "guide-on-the-side" model, advises Lynch. These younger attendees like to view themselves as participants who drive their own learning and have a great deal to add to the event conversation. In place of hierarchy is a more egalitarian, peer-to-peer, we're-all-in-this-together attitude. Give them a voice, or they will check out.

Trust also plays a key role in holding anyone's attention, but in different ways. When speaking to baby boomers, presenters have more leeway around when they get to the heart of their content takeaways. They can start slower in building their "relationship" with the audience and "bury the lead." Younger audiences usually expect the speaker to get to the meat of an idea, fast. They can be more transactional than relational.

So how can you truly engage your Millennials and Gen X audiences?

Try this, suggests Lynch. In advance of your event, email your participants your chosen speakers' talks in MP3 or video format. Allow or require attendees to watch the video or podcast of the speaker they're most drawn to before the event. Explain that when they arrive at the live shindig, they may choose which speaker they will join in person, as part of a small-group discussion with other attendees who favored that particular speaker.

This one simple change can bring about significant impacts, because you've turned the sage-on-the-stage into an interactive guide-on-the-side. Now, attendees become participants who play an integral role in the shape that their learning takes, with the speaker as their guide. Authentic, on-the-spot, collective interaction emerges organically from the meeting experience.

Five Non-Obvious Ways to Engage Audiences

With some background on the why, what and how of engagement, let's explore some non-obvious tools to engage attendees in ways that matter to them.

Tip 1 **Invite suspense writer John LaCarre to your event**

Ok, not literally. But you can set the stage for mystery, prestige and exclusivity by hinting at a new product reveal, a yet-to-be-named guest or the chance to be among the first to learn a new insight, solution or idea in your marketing material and messaging.

Tip 2 **Flip it**

Turn attendees into participants by changing who gets the most "air" time. Ask speakers to present in person for, say, fifteen minutes; follow this with forty-five minutes of time for *participants* to discuss *their* ideas, applications and strategies.

Tip 3 **Take a cue from Club Med**

How many ways can you position your event as a one-of-a-kind, exclusive group conclave? At registration, promote attendee-only Facebook groups. Intimate receptions with your headlining speaker. The chance to win a one-on-one coaching session with someone they admire. For early birds, front-row seats and other velvet-roped access throughout the event.

Tip 4 **Maximize investments in headlining speakers**

Host a VIP reception for those who generated the most "bring-a-friend" registrations or social media posts. The first fifty enrollees get an autographed book—or are entered into a drawing for the opportunity to dine with a top speaker and the executive team.

Tip 5 **Deliver networking at a NEW level**

A celebrated speaker and author of the book *Fascinate: How to Make Your Brand Impossible to Resist*, Sally Hogshead offers event planners a tool for building event buzz and buy-in days and weeks before participants arrive. As a reward for registering, attendees get free access to her quick, accurate assessment that reveals how they're individually fascinating. Upon arrival, name badges are adorned with ribbons printed with descriptions of each attendee's unique ability to fascinate. In no time, you set the stage for effortless networking and deeper learning—even before Sally walks on stage.

4.5 How to Use Music at Your Event

The song "Bohemian Rhapsody" by the band Queen is six minutes long. But I bet dollars to donuts that if you heard the first few chords of the song, you could recite the entire tune. Music is *that* powerful a means for engaging our whole selves and triggering deeply ingrained memories. Songs are also great as mnemonics, for fostering a sense of community and for generating feel-good hormones that engage our *whole* brain. If your events don't feature at least some music, you're cheating attendees of all these experiences. And you're neglecting ways to honor top performers, reinforce your most important messages, build cohesion, have (purposeful) fun, boost memory and even begin to change people's minds.

Need more evidence? Brain science geek alert. In *Stealing Fire,* the authors explain, "When listening to music, brainwaves move from the high-beta of normal waking consciousness down into the meditative (and trance-inducing) ranges of alpha and theta. At the same time, levels of stress hormones...drop, while social bonding and reward chemicals...spike. Add in entertainment—where people's brains synch to both the beat and to the brains of those around them—and you've got a potent combination for *communitas"* [an unstructured community in which people are equal].[10]

I believe so deeply in the importance of music at events that I've developed a deep bench of talent that delivers it in a broad range of forms: custom songs to recognize and reward employees, parody lyrics (performed live) set to tunes everyone knows that reflect an organization's culture. Songwriting and drumming workshops led by Grammy-nominated artists. Multimedia keynotes about what we can learn from the Beatles. Closing anthems that send everyone off on the highest possible note.

Groups with lower budgets integrate big-hit lip-synch contests, "name-that-tune" games that break up more serious programming and their own competitions in which teams vie to write the Best Song.

Important word of warning: If you want to play any type of musical work at your event, you may not simply click on the song in your iTunes folder (!). That's only for private use. At public events in the United States, copyrighted songs can only be played with a license at public events. Contact the three performing rights agencies to learn which holds the rights to the song(s) you plan to play. These include ASCAP, BMI and SESAC. *Or just hire a DJ.*

 ## How to Create a Winning Event Structure

It seems we all have some level of Attention Deficit Disorder. Dr. John Medina's data show that after only about ten minutes, our brains start losing their capacity to pay attention.[11] The antidote? Divide a session into ten-minute segments that differ in the ways information is presented. Follow, say, an expository segment with an emotion-laden story. Then include an interactive exercise to re-invigorate dulling brains. To be clear: I'm not suggesting you change up your *presenters* every ten minutes, but choose speakers who apply adult learning principles that can adjust the way information is delivered throughout a program.

Tip 1 **Ditch the platitudes, gratitudes and emphatitudes**

Right out of the gate, you make—or break—the success of an event. In the initial moments, audiences' attention spans are at their *highest* levels. And what almost always comes first in a show script? What I call platitudes and gratitudes: over-the-top thanking of people and sharing often-meaningless content. ACK!

The first cousins of platitudes and gratitudes? What event MC Brian Walter calls emphatitudes—platitudes stated emphatically.

Purveyors of emphatitudes are under the (utterly false) impression that if they just express their ideas with enough passion and VOLUME, they will more likely sway their audience's beliefs. That their words will make a stronger, more memorable impression. Instead, attendees can feel overwhelmed and disconnected. The meat of the message is muted, and the chance to communicate meaningfully is lost.

Not long ago, I attended a large, mission-critical, ninety-minute meeting that felt akin to witnessing a slow-motion train wreck. I painfully sat through the opening speaker's first ten minutes. It felt, and likely was, unscripted and seemingly without intent: "Good morning. I didn't hear you. GOOD MORNING! We are so excited you're here. Thank you. We appreciate you. We're here with our stakeholders. We're thrilled you're here. I want to thank our commissioners. We are excited about the work our CEO is doing..." That's 10% of the agenda hijacked! The only real impact of this? Everyone is bored.

What do you do instead of emphatitudes? It's up to you to obsess over these opening moments. Carefully script them with meaningful content. In place of the emphatitude ("We are a moonshot company. We reach for the stars!"), express specific, measurable and still-aspirational goals, like U.S. President John F. Kennedy did: "I believe that this nation should commit itself to achieving the goal, before this decade is out, of landing a man on the moon and returning him safely to the earth..."

Tip 2 **Recruit the whole mind**

Events that fully hit the mark engage all our senses. The spoken word is augmented with relevant visuals—created by speakers *and* by participants. The alluring aroma of food prepared right in front of attendees builds delicious, recallable memories of the moment. Read aloud, a customer's testimonial taps into our hard-wired love of story and community. Product demos spawn kinesthetic experiences that seal learning. Moments of surprise serve as multi-sensory hits, as surprise is scientifically proven to intensify our emotional experiences and boost recall. Song lyrics aren't just fun: they also help us remember, say, a new organizational mission.

Tip 3 **Level the field, literally**

Does your gathering require consensus building—a leveling of the playing field—to help reach a joint agreement? If so, then ensure there is no stage in the room so you keep all participants on the same level—literally. The conscious mind likely doesn't notice this set up, but the *subconscious* does.[12]

Tip 4 **Tell a story**

A well-designed event tells a unified, compelling story with a captivating arc and interesting characters, dialog and plot.

What story does your event tell? Does it have a clear and compelling *beginning*? *Plot twists* that create positive surprise? A suspenseful, clear and high-energy *conclusion*? What specific roles do each of your participants play in the telling of your organizational tale—before, during and after? We humans are wired for story-telling and story-listening.

A concluding chapter on storytelling: In designing your event's story arc, you generally want to open with programming that "speaks" to participants' left brains, builds over time with intellectual excitement, surprise and suspense, and closes with more personal, right-brain emotional messaging and content.

Tip 5 **Win, ping—and move to the next level**

Who doesn't like winning? Games engage by appealing to our competitive sides and involving multiple senses. Games are also a clear way to remind everyone about why they are together and what they have accomplished so far. At the very least, you can post an event checklist online or make written notes of clear milestones as you achieve them. As time goes on, show that you have, in fact, *overcome* hurdles: marketing plan for next year? DONE! Sensory rewards like the ring of a bell also make the accomplishment feel more real.

 # How to Engage Virtual Participants

It's hard enough to engage the participants sitting in front of you. What about those who tune in virtually? Let's discuss some non-obvious tools for engaging these "invisible" attendees at virtual or hybrid events (a hybrid event combines a live, in-person audience with a virtual audience). Keep in mind, many of these principles apply to boosting engagement at any gathering. (For a deeper dive into the challenges inherent in virtual communication, I recommend reading, *Can You Hear Me? How to Connect with People in a Virtual World*, by Nick Morgan.)

Tip 1 **Never choose the tech platform first**

When planning any type of virtual event component, some event organizers err in first choosing the technology to deliver the event to online viewers. (Facebook Live? Cisco WebEx? GoToWebinar? INXPO?

to name a few.) But professional conference moderator and MC Glenn Thayer notes that it's unwise to decide how the material will be delivered (your online "platform") before defining your content and format. This fences you in.[13] Instead, think about the content you want to communicate first, and then choose your platform, i.e. your content delivery technology. Television is an apt metaphor: If you were writing a sit-com, you'd first develop the script (content), and then design the set (platform).

Tip 2 **This is only a test**

Once technology is set, let online attendees experience a trial run. Send a test link through which registrants can try out the software and platform they'll use during the event itself.

Tip 3 **Event à la carte**

While designing the live and virtual agendas, know that your online attendees can have experiences distinct from what live attendees are having. For example: To keep your "invisible" (virtual) attendees maximally engaged, particularly if they've paid to join the event, give them a meaty, virtual-only Q&A session with your keynote speaker who conducts it off stage following the hybrid session, while live attendees move into something else. Doing so also helps boost your online viewership metrics.

Tip 4 **Social-eyes**

With so many social media tools available, it's tempting to use them all: Facebook, LinkedIn, Twitter, Google Hangouts, Skype, Instagram, ad infinitum. Narrow your choice by surveying where most attendees are naturally gathering and go to them, so the entire event is more impactful.

Tip 5 **"...And we're live..."**

If any part of your event is to be broadcast as a livestream, Thayer highly recommends hiring a broadcast producer. Armed with live television experience, this professional is responsible for consulting on and producing an event that's maximized for the needs of your livestream or virtual-feed audience, and that includes recommending the right lighting, sound and staging.

The broadcast producer can also make content recommendations. An example: At your live event, you've got a sponsor who's paid for the right to share remarks for seven minutes, from stage. Live attendees are in the room, so they're a captive audience. Not so much with your distractible virtuals—they'll check out with the speed of an animated GIF. Instead, put on your broadcast hat to produce a ROAR-ing, content-rich conversation or moderated Q&A between the event organizer's CEO and the sponsor around a timely subject that's relevant to the audience, the event host and the sponsor. Now you have all attendees paying attention to a topic that also puts the sponsor in its best light. For more tips on sponsorship strategies, see Chapter 7: How to Maximize Your Budget.

Tip 6 **Anyone got the time?**

If your virtual attendees are tuning in from more than a couple of time zones, be mindful of early or late start times. 10 A.M. on the East Coast is about as early as you want to start an event that includes West Coasters, for example. Speaking of timing, keep all your virtual segments to no more than sixty minutes in length, total. And livestream and hybrid events—like our favorite TV shows—must *start and end right on time.*

Tip 7 **Please release me**

If you plan to capture any video footage or photographs, your participants must sign a release to grant permission. Most event organizers simply address this in the terms and conditions people agree to when they register.

Tip 8 **The boring vs. ROAR-ing opener**

Thayer suggests that you *begin* a hybrid event (and any event!) with your very best, most enticing content. (Hint: this is NOT sponsors' remarks or the welcoming of a new board president!)

These are platitudes and gratitudes. Your juiciest content should lead the way to *grab* everyone's attention—and *keep* it til the end. So, *dive right in* to your most compelling ideas. This also positions your event as unmissable, and if you're recording the programming, it ensures that the footage can be maximally used in a promotional teaser for the next event ("See what you missed?!").

Boring: "Thank you for joining us at the 23rd Annual South-Central Economics Summit! You're in for a great two days. And without our corporate partners, we wouldn't even be here..."

ROAR-ing: "Across the world, in this time of political and fiscal upheaval, economic and monetary policy has never mattered more. Your presence and participation over the next two days are crucial in our collective efforts to establish market-stabilizing strategies. Let's begin..."

Tip 9 **Let's just hang out**

After your virtual or hybrid event, hold virtual meet-ups online (via Google Hangouts, Zoom, Facebook Live etc.) so any attendee (real or virtual) can continue to connect, learn and network. Doing so will also boost in-person attendance over time as relationships crystallize.

Tip 10 **Data-driven results**

An inherent benefit of virtual events is that you can easily track virtual attendance, click-through rates, retention, which content most resonated and more. Take advantage of this built-in ROI data so you can quantify your value for stakeholders and decide what improvements to make to your next events.

(For tools and inspiration for extending engagement after your event, see Chapter 15: Encore! Encore!)

CHAPTER SUMMARY:
THREE THINGS TO REMEMBER

→ If attendees don't participate in co-creating content that matters to them, we have failed as event organizers, and everyone may as well stay home.

→ How we gain attention varies by generation: 50+ generally accept top-down, passive ways of absorbing information. Younger audiences want to more actively drive their own learning in peer-to-peer environments.

→ To ensure maximum attention levels, begin all in-person and hybrid events with your very best, most enticing, carefully scripted content—and never start with sponsor-related remarks or the welcoming of VIPs.

PART TWO

Techniques

CHAPTER 5

How to Curate a Kick-Ass Speaker Lineup

The right speaker, with the right message, at the right time, will drive event buzz, boost registration, ignite a movement, move the dial on your most important initiatives and foster longtime event memories for everyone present.

The wrong speaker will suck the life out of your event, harm your reputation, alienate stakeholders and bore people to death.

(No pressure.)

Ah, but lucky you! We've got you covered. Whether for your programming you rely on subject matter experts from your industry, and/or you invite paid speakers, performers or celebrities to present, this chapter will give you a reliable road map that saves you time, money, guesswork and aspirin.

Throughout my thirty-year career, I've been aligning relevant speakers, hosts, celebrities, entertainers, comedians and trainers with corporate, trade association and public audiences to help people learn what they need to be more effective in the world. This is my jam, man!

Every day, I'm in the trenches of adult learning, And, as a longtime member in the International Association of Speakers' Bureaus and recipient of its Pacesetters Award for bringing more innovation to the events industry, I have seen what works and what doesn't.

These days, there are more speakers in the marketplace than ever before. The TED revolution has played a catalytic role in increasing exposure for the spoken word and offering a shining example of how to present expertise effectively.

As a result, today's audiences expect original ideas to be presented in clear, concise and entertaining ways.

So, how can you sort through the ever-growing rosters of speakers to land on the one or five who will slay it for you?

Do not assume that
the more speakers you
consider for a particular
slot, the more likely you are
to find the right one.

This is simply not true. In fact, I believe that just the
opposite is true. Fewer, carefully selected choices equate
with better outcomes (a principle based on decades of
experience with groups who've tried this, and addressed
in Barry Schwartz' seminal book, *The Paradox of Choice:
Why More Is Less*). This concept has never been as
applicable to the speaking world as it is now, with so
many presenters to choose from. Shorten your list to
choose wisely.

Don't rely on a large committee of volunteers and peers to generate speaker, entertainer and/or host recommendations.

Here's why: Just because someone is affiliated with your organization doesn't mean he or she is ideally suited to provide the most informed guidance on content curation. Sometimes I work with groups who have assembled a multi-tabbed spreadsheet with dozens of speaker options that the committee finds interesting, for whatever reason. These many committee members often identify prospective speakers based solely on their personal interests rather than a strategy.

Identifying speaker options this way is, well, backwards, and needlessly time consuming. In place of trying to compile exhaustive lists of potential presenters, the non-obvious and ever-more-effective path is to replace volume with strategy. It's time to get crystal clear on what you want your paid and pro-bono speakers to deliver. The more granular the better.

5.1 The Four-Question Strategy for Identifying Ideal Speakers

In Chapter 1, I offered you four questions to ask to take events from bore to ROAR (what I call Return On Attendee Relevance). Likewise, landing on a final, finely tuned and fabulous speaker lineup requires a proven question-and-answer-driven strategy to get at the heart of what your attendees want and need to succeed.

I call these **The Why Behind the Who** strategy questions that reveal your event's content objectives. Indeed, this Q&A is similar to the bore-to-ROAR question strategy presented earlier. Together, these Why Behind the Who questions generate what I call **The Content Map.**

The Content Map is your ace-in-the-hole tool for sorting through the haystack of experts to find those few precious needles. It's your event throughline.

These four questions will generate your map:

Question 1 **What do we want the audience to think, feel, do and/or believe as a result of this event? (Name the outcomes.)**

In the same way that this question will guide you in your overall event design, it's also very helpful when selecting a speaker. The question forces you to begin with the end in mind.

For example, maybe you ultimately want to move the organization from #2 in the marketplace to #1. And to do so, you must lower customer attrition rates, become a "best place to work," or maybe acquire their top competitor.

If the goal is to achieve a *motivational* shift in the audience, then specify what the participants need to be *motivated to do differently*. For example, perhaps they need to earn a top safety designation by cutting on-the-job accidents by 15%. The more detailed the goals around the mental shifts you want to foster, the better.

Question 2 **If we could invite any smarty-pants pre-senter—dead or alive—who would we choose? (Generate a fresh perspective that ultimately inspires "get-able" speakers within budget.)**

This question moves you into a sense of possibility and big-picture thinking, and your responses can then inform your search for speakers who align with your budget and timeline.

Question 3 **What will we do at our event that can only be experienced in a *live* setting? (Aim for interaction and engagement.)**

As noted in Chapter 1, asking this question early in the event-design process allows us to more easily bake in moments and formats that make the most of face-to-face, co-created experiences that involve listening, dialog, trust building, empathy and collaboration.

Question 4 **Our featured speaker(s) just completed the session(s) and the event is over. All attendees are departing together, on a bus. What comments is the bus driver overhearing about their experiences?**

Drafting these "bus driver's comments" will help you determine what success looks like in your speaker lineup, as they shine bright headlights on the kinds of presenters you're looking for. Starting with the end in mind, you'll more effectively reach your content goals.

Using my distinct Why Behind the Who Q&A process, you should now have a clear map of the takeaways and outcomes you want your internal and external presenters to achieve.

Here's a simple sample of what a specific event's content could look like on the Map:

The Content Map

FIND THE WHY BEHIND YOUR WHO

A proven question-and-answer strategy to determine your event's critical outcomes, experience set and content scope. **It's your event throughline.**

What do we want the audience to think, feel, do, and/or believe as a result of this event? (Name the outcomes.) In this example, the audience is a group of executives and managers at a healthcare company.

1

THINK: Innovation isn't scary; innovation and disruption begin at the level of the individual to help built a more innovative culture.

FEEL: Inspired to innovate to improve products, services and processes; empowered to uncover fresh, actionable ideas.

DO: Take learnings from this event back to employee teams and discuss ways that each person is integral to idea generation; as a group, write an action plan together showing specific steps each department will take this quarter; decide how we will encourage and award " fast failure."

BELIEVE: Everyone is a capable innovator on whom the future of our organization depends.

If we could invite any smarty-pants presenter - dead or alive - who would we choose? (Generate a fresh perspective that ultimately inspires "get-able" speakers within budget.)

2

Jeff Bezos, CEO of Amazon

What will we do at our event that can only be experienced in a live setting? (Aim for the interaction and engagement.)

3

After speaker's keynote, invite everyone to participate in a Gamestorming-style innovation session, led by our speaker, to identify, evaluate and prioritize potential markets for innovation; examine and rethink our strategic focus and plan a future roadmap.

Our featured speaker(s) just completed the session(s) and the event is over. All attendees are departing together, on a bus. What comments is the bus driver overhearing about their experiences? (Determine what success looks like across the entire event.)

4

"I used to think innovation only came from light bulb moments. Now I see it's really about careful observation and purposeful iteration." "Knowing what specifically drives innovation within a corporate culture helps me see where I fit into that process and what I can do to move the needle." "Our best offsite event to date because everyone was involved in a conversation we really were hungry for."

Use the Content Map anytime you need to gain a clear path to your event's critical outcomes, experience set and content scope.

DOWNLOAD TEMPLATE

To download your own content map template, visit our online resources area.

5.2 Where to Find Great Speakers

Now that you're equipped with your map, it's time to start identifying presenters who align with this plan.

Where will you find your best-suited speakers?

Tip 1 **Seek out experts on experts**

27,300,000. That's how many results are generated in a web search for "customer service speaker." Don't have time to sort through that number? Didn't think so. When I see event organizers overwhelmed, struggling with finding and vetting speakers on their own, I am all the more convinced of the value that speakers' bureaus offer.

So, take your trusty Content Map to your favorite bureau, and get a list of tailored speaker recommendations. After all, these are experts on experts, whose full-time job is having ready access to the best talent and topics for events like yours. You'll save time, guesswork and worry—often without paying more.

Here's why:

Most agencies are compensated with a commission from each booked speaker's fee, and often the speaker's fee is the same whether you book through the bureau or directly with the speaker.

And since time is money, typically agencies, bureaus and speaker management companies will drastically reduce or eliminate almost all the labor-intensive, pre- and post-contract communication between you and speaker prospects, write the offer to the speaker, submit the contract, handle the speaker's logistics and schedule a debrief. And just like that, you free up loads of time for many other event-planning tasks. (See Chapter 12: How to Plan an Event on (Almost) Any Timeline for more details.)

A word of warning: My distinct approach is to act as an agent on behalf of event planners, going out into the entire universe of speakers, entertainers and MCs to find the best matches. I don't broker a specific set of speakers from an exclusive roster. Be sure you understand your bureau's loyalties before making your choices.

Tip 2 **TED and TEDx**

Unless you've just emerged from a multi-year retreat in the mountains of Bhutan, you're familiar with TED and TEDx. Nearly every day of the year, this organization and its licensed affiliates host live events around the world that feature short, expertly curated talks that crack viewers' curious heads open on everything from the beauty behind math, spaghetti sauce (and what it has to do with choice and happiness) to how to permanently end war. Plus, TED's eighteen-minute-max format is salve for shrinking attention spans and can be an effective way to share novel ideas and present unexpected insights in a short amount of time.

The good news and the bad news: There are now thousands of TED and TEDx speakers roaming the planet, and many are looking for more speaking gigs. As these folks are busy thought leaders, you may find it difficult to sort through, reach and book them. As with any speaker worth your audience's time, I recommend enlisting help from an agency in securing a TED or TEDx speaker to make your booking process more efficient and effective.

(For more on TED, read Chapter 10: How to Think Like a TED Conference Organizer.)

Tip 3 **Celebrity speakers and entertainers**

The larger your event budget, the more likely you may invite a buzz-generating "big name" or two to your gathering.

A note of caution: The higher you go up the "celebrity food chain," the less likely speakers and entertainers will tailor their remarks for your audience. And some will only present in a moderated Q&A format. If that's ok with you, then go for it.

Be sure you know what you're getting—and not getting. Regardless of the speakers you choose, I recommend that you note *everything* you want that speaker or entertainer to do in your written offer.

This is especially crucial at the celebrity level. Your offer should include elements like the specified length of the speaker's talk, conditions for travel reimbursements, social media posts and mainstream media interviews on your behalf, a video recording of the talk (and how you will use any edited footage) and any VIP reception you plan to host. Whatever you value and expect, put it in writing. Attempts to add such asks after contracting will almost surely backfire.

Tip 4 **Referrals from peers and other organizers**

Make the most of your conversations with peers and colleagues by asking for as many specifics as possible. What did the presenter do for your group? What was the result? How deeply was the content customized? What else was in the contract beyond, say, a keynote?

Tip 5 **Is your RFP an RFF (Request for Frustration)?**

If your organization uses Requests for Proposals to help fill speaker slots, I suggest using a mechanism that ensures your final roster of speakers truly aligns with what you have deemed to be your most important goals, in the sense that they are most *relevant* to your attendees. I've seen too many RFPs with requests so broad that selection committees are overwhelmed not only by *quantity*, but by lack of *quality*. There's more bore than ROAR.

To convert frustration into fruition, put all details about expectations and compensation in the publicly facing material so you get fewer, but better, choices. Remember to heed the Paradox of Choice!

 5.3 # How to Vet Your Speakers

Once you've established your prospective speaker lineup, it's time to vet your short list (and oh, for your sake, I hope the list is short-ish!). Here are some tried-and-true (and non-obvious) tips for evaluating presenters—whether paid or unpaid.

Tip 1 **Watch the videos**

Of course, you're going to check out the sizzle reels that presenters put on their websites. But in a world seemingly blanketed in YouTube footage, take your vetting deeper by searching for more of their talks on the web, and take time to watch longer recordings to see how the speaker's entire story arc unfolds. You can also ask for footage of a full-length talk.

Tip 2 **See them present live**

When possible, ask the speaker if you can attend a live session as a guest. This is an ideal way to experience both the content and the energy speakers bring to a room.

Tip 3 **Go beyond TED Talks**

TED and TEDx speakers practice their five- to eighteen-minute talks for months, have almost always committed their remarks to memory and are often extensively coached. Doesn't that make them all shoe-ins for your forty-five- to ninety-minute keynote slot?

Not so fast.

When it comes to inviting TED and TEDx speakers, fellow speakers' bureau owner Brian Palmer warns: "Don't assume that speakers who are great at delivering an eighteen-minute talk to a TED audience will be equally great at delivering a sixty-minute keynote to your particular group, which may be looking for a type of presentation that doesn't align with the typical TED Talk."[14]

So, what to do instead? Vet a TED speaker as you would any other—and watch some of their non-TED speaking videos. If they don't have any videos besides a TED Talk, vet more carefully and ask more questions.

Tip 4   **Inquire about interactivity**

Ask prospective presenters what the audience will do while they present. If they say, "Well, they will listen to me speak," take this as your cue to find a different speaker if interaction is paramount (and I hope you've come to see the crucial value of such interaction by this point in the book). For an evolving list of speakers who deliver exceptionally interactive sessions, visit: http://www.nomoreboringmeetings.com/interactive-speakers

5.4   How to Prepare Speakers for Success

Regardless of the mix of subject matter experts, generalists, paid and unpaid speakers, hosts and facilitators that you employ for your event, you will elevate the quality of your event when you schedule what I call a Message Continuity Conference Call in advance of your event. Here's how it works.

Gather everyone with a stake in event messaging, such as internal presenters from your organization as well as your external, hired keynote speaker(s). Ask each one to share two to three of their main points and takeaways with the whole group. Then listen for ways they can reinforce one another.

For example, is the CEO discussing a key revenue growth initiative? Then how can your outside keynote speaker whose story centers on teaming and cohesion strengthen the executive's remarks? It could be as simple as using the growth initiative as an example of the crucial role that team cohesion plays in reaching it.

In bringing everyone together in a real-time conversation ahead of your event, you ensure that patterns emerge in the content, which amplifies the impact of the overall event theme. This call also ensures that contradictions or conflicting messages are identified and cleared up in advance.

To avoid information overload, increase your attendees' retention and increase your return on investment, center your focus on two or three takeaways.

Share your content map with your speakers and host.

This will help them understand your overarching event objectives, reinforce your programming vision and deliver on your most critical messaging.

5.5 Bring on the SMEs, Please

You might augment your professional speaker lineup with subject matter experts (SMEs) from your industry or you may rely completely on SMEs for all your event programming. Either way—and like it or not—your audience is comparing an SME's delivery to that of a professional, paid speaker. And they are likely seeing a substantial discrepancy between the two.

After all, becoming an expert in something does not require knowing how to present on it.

But if you want your SMEs to shine, and your participants to walk away satisfied and with clear takeaways, it's time you help your expert presenters learn how to deliver their deep knowledge effectively in ways the audience *wants* to hear it.

No one is born with this skill, but it can—and I believe must—be learned by any thought leader who wants to be worth his or her reputation.

My go-to resource for training in this arena is National Speakers Association Hall of Fame inductee and communication consultant Brian Walter.

Walter's live and virtual "Don't Break Your Breakout" sessions show SMEs how to unlearn ineffective habits: Cramming in too much information. Relying too heavily on slide decks and data. Focusing more on themselves and what they know and not enough on what the audience needs. Delivering material that's short on big-aha insights, yet long on length. Failing to adequately rehearse.

On the other hand, the best SMEs—those who don't break their breakouts!—place the spotlight on the *audience,* integrate cutting-edge storytelling with insights from their own experiences, avoid data dumping and practice adequately. The result: highly engaging, actionable and memorable sessions.

DOWNLOAD TEMPLATE

Learn about "Don't Break Your Breakout" here: http://www.nomoreboringmeetings.com/portfolio_page/dont-break-your-breakout/

CHAPTER SUMMARY:
THREE THINGS TO REMEMBER

→ The most effective way to identify best-fit speakers is to replace volume with strategy via my four Why Behind the Who questions and Content Map that reveal your event's top content objectives.

→ Time- and aspirin-saving sources for speaker selection include experts on experts (AKA speakers' bureaus), TED and TEDx rosters and referrals from peers.

→ Professional speakers and SMEs adept at interacting meaningfully with participants will generate deeper learning and more kick-ass results.

CHAPTER 6

How to Use Panels, Q&A Sessions and Event Hosts

Many event producers augment programming with panel discussions and question-and-answer segments. While panels and Q&As can be superb, they're usually suboptimal and predictable, short on insights and long on length, unmoored and formulaic.

Wouldn't you rather offer engaging dialogs, memorable interplay, tangible takeaways, friendly arguments, authentic debate and purposeful experiences whose sums are greater than their parts?

Your audiences would like that, too.

 ## 6.1 How to Produce More Powerful Panels

A key strategy to transform your panels from bore to ROAR is to ensure panelists deliver remarks from the audience's point of view. While you will of course choose panelists because they have specific, valuable points of view, whatever the moderator asks and however panelists respond must be in service of each event's particular audience.

For example, this point of view is in service of the panelist: "When I was a top consultant at McKinsey, we showed our retail clients how to integrate Internet of Things technology into existing business models faster than any other firm."

This comment is in service of the audience:

> *"The Internet of Things is constantly evolving. Given everyone here is in agriculture, the most important step is use a secure IoT framework for building your ecosystem. I'll send a URL for a whitepaper on that..."*

A great panel-based conversation starts with carefully crafted questions. Be sure whoever leads the way in getting a conversation started has a broad view of the issues your audience cares about, so the resulting banter fully hits the mark.

Also, just because you have a moderator and panelists on stage, doesn't mean you can't include those who are off stage. Involve your audience in a panel by asking for their questions in advance (or in real time), and/ or breaking up panelists' input by giving the audience at least one opportunity to discuss a question among themselves, 1:1 or in small groups (a panel within a panel!).

**DOWNLOAD:
RESOURCE**

For a deep dive on producing great panels— everything from curating panelists to choosing AV to extending the experience after your event—check out www.PowerfulPanels.com and the book by the same name by Kristin Arnold.

6.2 How to Improve Your Event Q&A

Question-and-answer sessions, just like panels, can engage and inform—or they can career off the rails.

Savvy event organizers know not to leave such programming to chance. Let's explore non-obvious practices for Q&A so that all your future sessions sizzle.

Tip 1 **Lay the groundwork**

First, and most importantly, let the presenters who will be taking Q&A know that you stage "Best Practice Q&A" and as such, you don't want to *end* the entire program with Q&A.

Instead, ask them—in advance of the event so they can thoughtfully prepare—to close with a final, short and relevant point, anecdote or big-picture insight.

Think of your sessions as a content sandwich: Main program, Q&A, short closing segment.

This three-part package unites all the remarks in a memorable, positive way. If you *end* with Q&A, you have no control over how your events end, how attendees depart or the last emotions and thoughts you leave with audiences. After all, what if the last question sucks the air right out of the room? Is confrontational?

Drones on and on? Instead, give your *speakers* and panelists the last word, and enjoy positive conclusions to events you work so hard to design.

Tip 2 **Run with it**

Prepare to have runners in the aisles who deliver cordless mic(s) to those wishing to ask questions. Or have a couple mics on stands at the front of the room.

Tip 3 **Prepare your audience**

Ask your presenter to say something like this—and note that each component is integral to your success: "That concludes my main remarks. As you know, we've included a short Q&A in this session. It will last fifteen minutes. I'll then close with final remarks. So that we can maximize our time together, please keep your question short, and *in the form of a question*, so that we can address as many questions as possible with the time allotted. Also...please, 1. Raise your hand, 2. *Wait for a mic to come to you* and 3. State your question. Who wishes to go first?"

Tip 4 **Use a proven answer protocol**

Whether the question was amplified or not, be sure the presenter repeats or summarizes each question so everyone can hear it. Those who don't hear the question certainly won't be engaged in the answer. Then have presenters share short, relevant answers to address each question while allowing as much participation and engagement as possible.

Tip 5 **Plant a plant**

If you think questions will be minimal, or politically charged, appoint someone in the audience to ask the first question. Yes, folks: a plant. This is your "safety net" who delivers a thoughtful, pre-selected question that sets a positive tone for the rest of the Q&A.

Tip 6 **Employ a crucial, strategic close**

When there's time for one more question, ask the speaker to inform participants so they can know what to expect. And if the speaker is willing, and it's clear that questions still remain, announce that the speaker will linger to take questions 1:1 after the program is over.

Tip 7 **End on a high note**

Then, the speaker presents a pre-selected closing vignette to wrap up the program.

Voilà: You've stayed on track, maintained crucial levels of engagement and informed your audience with new insights.

You can also breathe new life into Q&A segments by giving them fresh names like "Hot Seat" or "Ask Me Anything" and inviting your leadership or panelists to the stage to take any question thrown at them.

ACK! Q&A is not engagement.

While a well-designed Q&A session will positively augment your agenda, it's not synonymous with true audience engagement.

You may have had this experience: You ask speakers how they'll interact with attendees, and some say, "I'll add Q&A at the end." As if that will solve the problem.

It will not. **It's a lazy solution.**

Including a Q&A session does not equal automatic audience engagement.

Sure...a handful of folks may feel engaged when the speaker answers *their* questions. But the rest? They're often tuned out, as "the Qs" being asked are, at best, moderately interesting to the broader group, and at worst, completely irrelevant.

Just like that, you've committed a bore crime.

So, what can you do in place of Q&A, or to supplement it? Try the format options in Chapter 8: Unconventional Event Formats, and my Post-Program Pair-Up concept in Chapter 15: Encore! Encore!

 ## How to Elevate the Impact of Your Event Host

Almost all events, except the most informal, require a master or mistress of ceremonies, a conference weaver, an event facilitator, a learning coach or an interstitial energizer. (And yes, these are all really synonyms for host!) If your event is a fundraiser, you'll need an auctioneer.

No matter what you call the person in this role, you can maximize the impact by **hiring a professional host.** If you can't afford to pay your speakers, you must smash the piggy bank to pay a professional host (rather than, say, rely on that really outgoing colleague in accounting or whomever else you've pegged to do the deed for free).

Yep, even the most cash-strapped event organizers are wise to prioritize hiring a great host—the role is that pivotal. Here's why.

Your host is often delivering the very first interaction, energy and content that your audience experiences at your event. Any gaffe here has a disproportionately negative impact on your entire event, since we all know first impressions matter most.

In addition to telling people about the restrooms, the schedule and the location of the coffee, a seasoned host provides a red thread of professionalism and insightful connections—"agenda glue" placed between your program elements that helps spur memories and boost recall.

Ideally, they are compensated for preparing thoroughly and for contributing informed comments that help generate a sense of meaning and foster connections among all your sessions. Collectively, their input forms a powerful, pattern-rich tapestry of otherwise overwhelming and possibly disjointed programming.

They don't simply phone it in with meaningless comments like: "Wow, Jezebel, that was an amazing talk! Now, let's take a break." Rather, they've done their homework to build deep awareness of each presenter's remarks, and leverage what they hear during the live event. Then, your audience will hear meaty, useful, actionable connective tissue: "Jezebel's story about how she slayed the dragon should give our sales team a frame of reference and tools for prospects' objections. Her resolution also reinforces what Ms. CEO said in her opening video around our capacity for meeting our financial objectives in Q3. Let's break into groups to practice...."

WHAT THE MOST EXCEPTIONAL EVENT HOSTS DO...

→ **Channel the prowess and polish of Jimmy Fallon or Ellen DeGeneres.** These famous TV hosts got that way and are beloved by gajillions because they always put their guests in their best light. They keep the spotlight *off* themselves and on the participants, and deliver charm, wit and playfulness by the bucketful. Guests' on-stage stress is lessened, and they can show up more authentically. I recently sat in an event audience, and to my horror, the MC thought he was the star of the show. Not only did he YELL! EVERY! WORD! (another woman and I actually plugged our ears to lower the volume!), he also interjected while someone else had the mic to share an irrelevant tidbit of knowledge. *Gah!*

→ **Ensure that the presenter knows how to pronounce every name, acronym and insider term— in advance.** Does Patti Smith actually pronounce her name Patti "Smythe"? If an industry acronym is MDAC, is it pronounced "M-DAC" or "M-D-A-C"? In Washington State, your MC will be an instant hero for correctly pronouncing Puyallup. Such details matter to the audience, and they matter to professional, prepared MCs as well.

→ **Read scripted remarks conversationally,** and interject thoughtful, respectful, extemporaneous observations along with clean humor.

→ **Bring technical prowess,** including awareness about staging and production, along with the capacity to troubleshoot audio-visual snags.

To uncover great host choices in a methodical way, refer to my speaker-selection methodology in Chapter 5: How to Curate a Kick-Ass Speaker Lineup. And for more background on staging best-in-class virtual events, check out the "How to Engage Virtual Participants" section in Chapter 4: Why You Need More Engagement.

CHAPTER SUMMARY:
THREE THINGS TO REMEMBER

→ The most engaging, insight-rich panels and Q&A sessions are not left to chance—they're thoughtfully produced.

→ If a panel or Q&A is the only time when your audience will interact with your speaker(s), you have committed a bore crime; Q&A does not equal audience engagement.

→ If you spend cash nowhere else, invest it in a professional host who purposefully keeps the event moving, and provides critical "agenda glue" between program elements and helps participants boost recall.

CHAPTER 7

How to Maximize Your Budget

Do you have an unlimited budget?

Didn't think so. In this chapter we'll focus on straightforward, powerful, non-obvious ways to save some shekels, secure more dynamic sponsorships and squeeze more value from other event elements.

Let's explore some fresh ways to boost sponsorship funds through strategy and experience brandin.g

When it comes to sponsorships, a memory from a trade association meeting is locked in my mind. I recall the head of sponsorships was talking to the crowd about the value of serving as a financial partner. The pitch? "We need money." It was that un-subtle. Other organizations (maybe yours?) may soften the language a bit, but likely your messaging is *more about you than it is about whom you're trying to woo.*

Indeed, if your events or tradeshows rely on sponsorship dollars, you can drastically improve both how meeting goers engage with sponsors *and* improve the results sponsors gain from their fiscal partnerships with you. You can become a master or mistress of the *smart-per-ship!*

In my efforts leading the TEDxSeattle sponsorship team, the most important goal in attendee-sponsor interactions is to offer cool experiences that *attendees* care about, with very little perceptible focus on sponsors' marketing messages.

In other words, we aim to integrate relevant messaging and moments that people want to hear and experience rather than interrupt them with what can only be perceived as annoying advertising.

Aptly, in marketing parlance, this is called **experience branding.**

Focusing on what audiences care about, we *auto-magically* create a **triple win**: more buy-in from participants, more palpable engagement among attendees and sponsors, and as a result, better bottom-line results for sponsors.

How to Secure the Right Sponsors

Laying the groundwork for this triple win demands you move beyond the old-school, obvious game of "logo soup." In other words, if you just offer sponsors logo placement, don't be surprised if all you hear is crickets. Instead, think: creative, customized and colorless (i.e. no more gold-silver-bronze levels; those became un-hip years ago).

To that end, here are seven tips to whet your appetite:

Tip 1 **Start early**

Know your prospects' fiscal calendars and plan accordingly. Reach out at least nine months ahead, preferably more, or budgets may already be allocated.

Tip 2 **Stand in your sponsors' shoes**

No one is waiting, check in hand, to hear from you.
If only! You've got to come to the table having done
your homework. Understand your prospects' reasons
for partnering with organizations. Their values. Their
missions. And then make a strategic marketing case
for your value proposition. Most companies seeking
sponsorship these days want to boost brand awareness;
engage, in real time, with prospective customers; build
community and social impact; showcase new offerings
in unexpected ways; and recruit top performing
employees. Be sure all your communications speak
first to each company's needs and goals. Also realize
that your sponsor's investment isn't just the monies
you receive. They must also factor in the costs of
sponsorship activation: costs such as marketing
collateral, staffing and product distribution.

Tip 3 **Add value and offer choice**

For $x to $y investment, allow your sponsor to choose
from, say, five experience branding options. Or
integrate a way to begin engaging with your audience
as soon as your contract is signed (i.e. before the
event), and three months after the event. And/or offer a
discount for locking in sponsorship at multiple events.

Tip 4 **Fall in love with data**

The more you know and communicate to prospective sponsors about your audience demographics, the more companies you'll find that align with your event. Is yours an audience of female coders? Yoga lovers? BMX enthusiasts? Active retirees? How many, what ages, what income and education levels? Offers for sponsorship become more valuable when you can both quantify, in detail, your audience reach and demographics, and deliver a comprehensive report of audience engagement data your partner will receive after the event. And, be sure to make use of a tool that provides metrics on audience engagement. Whether it's reach on social media, metrics tied to shares from your photo booth, or customer activations from coupon codes, quantify and share these numbers with your valued fiscal friends.

Tip 5 **Be, um, non-obvious!**

The most visible companies and brands are inundated with requests for sponsorship—sometimes dozens a day. At an event I worked on, we had a hard time getting a response from ubiquitous Starbucks, but

Stumptown—a smaller, but worthy competitor—courted us. For every large company, there are smaller (less obvious) options to uncover.

Tip 6 **Attend events your top sponsor prospects are supporting—and pay attention**

Take time to exprience for yourself how other organizations create value for sponsor companies you are courting. This will give you more ideas on the types of audience engagement experiences that most appeal to them. And then you can include at least some of these proven elements in your proposal, so next time they choose to partner with you.

Tip 7 **Save money on travel expenses**

Think beyond a cash infusion and look to travel companies for travel vouchers and related in-kind donations instead of sponsorship in the form of money. Note too that only some speakers will accept flight vouchers for their air travel.

7.2

Examples of Winning Sponsorships

Well-aligned sponsors will support your desire to produce one-of-a-kind event experiences while they benefit from exposure to your audience. The following mini-case studies are examples of audience-driven interactions that reinforce that *when attendees win, everyone wins.*

→ **Starbucks and the Seattle Seahawks** scored a game-winning touchdown when they staged a charity drive (in line with their community-building values) with Seahawks head coach Pete Carroll and eight of his players. The Seahawks took over the coffee counter at a neighborhood Starbucks and served coffee to eager, caffeine-craving fans. The result: lines out the door, loads of social media engagement and plenty of good will for all.

→ **At TEDxSeattle,** we worked with our top-level partner in the financial services industry to build custom interactive experiences where attendees interact with content related to the overall event theme, the speakers' takeaways and ideas that matter to attendees themselves—like their own financial wellbeing. Tchotchkes and promotional fliers are nowhere to be found. The result? The partner considers the value of this partnership "immeasurable," and comes back year after year.

→ **Adobe was a sponsor at TEDActive**. Rather than stage a predictable "old-school" photo booth via which they distributed, say, literature and software downloads, they designed a novel way for participants to experience how drawing leads to deeper creativity. Using Adobe software, attendees were led through fun exercises that allowed them to see why they didn't need to be Rembrandt to create something beautiful.

→ **At a rodeo,** VIPs got to see how dirt for the arena was brought in, which was an experience supported with sponsorship dollars. Such exclusive, behind-the-scenes, "backstage" experiences make special events more special, and are fascinating for niche groups. What's your event's equivalent of rodeo dirt?!

→ **A shoe polish brand** paid cash for the opportunity to set up shoeshine booths during an event that predominantly targeted men. What similar under-the-radar sponsorship opportunities can you uncover?

→ Involve a number of brands in a sponsored **hangover kit** and distribute it the morning after a company party. Funny, practical, memorable and buzz-worthy.

→ It's common to secure sponsors who subsidize the cost of external presenters. Try instead a non-obvious approach that creates an even bigger win and can enhance your relationship with the sponsor. **Negotiate with your speaker a second, separate session** at a local school while she's in town for your event. Ta-da!—you just scored a win-win-win-win: You secure a great speaker, your sponsor's basks in a spotlight that supports their educational or social-action mission, your audience gets a great experience and a group of school kids is inspired by the presenter's message, too.

→ At TED itself, activewear company **lululemon sponsored a meditation and quiet room.** Another group took this idea further by finding sponsors for different stations strewn around the event venue, with each station featuring low-cost essential oil diffusers that released scents to help attendees destress and boost mental clarity.

→ What if you **offer your sponsors exclusive access** to otherwise hard-to-access executives as part of their packages?

→ A technology firm aiming to create more awareness for its latest offerings and its social responsibility efforts paid to **play a slide deck during event breaks** that visually showcased "5 things you didn't know about _____ company," interspersed with fun trivia questions. This was a low-key but information-rich way for event goers to learn of their sponsors' good works.

(For another audience-driven example of showcasing a sponsor, see the sponsor success story sidebar in Chapter 10: How to Think Like a TED Conference Organizer.)

 ## How to Negotiate a Discount from Speakers

If you've applied my *Why Behind the Who* and Content Map methodology in Chapter 5: How to Curate a Kick-Ass Speaker Lineup, you now have a list of top speaker choices whom you've carefully vetted. But you're not so sure you can afford 'em. So, **what can you offer your preferred speaker(s) in exchange for a full fee?**

→ **Rob Peter to pay Paul.** Sometimes the difference between the speaker you really want and the speaker you think you can afford is the difference between feeding attendees chicken vs. steak. Changing one menu item could free up funds for the speaker you really want.

→ Ask if any of your speakers' content is re-search-based. If so, the presentation and the results it generates at your event could be the basis of a future case study, giving you some fee leverage if the speaker can **turn your event into a research study.**

→ If the speaker has authored a book or has products, make a bulk book or product buy and **hold a book**

signing (save more money, of course, by having attendees buy the books).

→ Offer the option to **video record the session** in exchange for promotional use of the footage.

→ Offer to **send a branded gift from your speaker** to your mail list of attendees. (As noted in Chapter 15: Encore! Encore!, according to Event Marketer, 74% of attendees feel more positively about a brand or product that's promoted after they've attended an event.)

→ **Introduce the speaker to a few of your industry colleagues** who are known for paying their speakers well.

→ Arrange for a reporter to **interview your speaker and publish the story** on a media channel he/she covets.

→ **Cover the cost for the speaker's family to attend** your destination event (perhaps through a sponsor?).

→ **Expand the scope:** Many top-tier speakers' fees are "inclusive." That is, one fee includes the presentation fee and travel and you won't be surprised by unexpectedly high travel costs when the event is over. Some will be amendable to conducting an added breakout, participating in a panel, attending a VIP reception or hosting a banquet for marginally more. Others might include signed books. Stay curious, get creative and negotiate wisely.

→ Busy authors like to maximize their time, so try to **align with another date on a book tour** and possibly get leverage in your fee negotiation. Most authors on book tour post their schedules on websites or their publisher's websites. While you'll likely be unable to work very far in advance (weeks or a few months, tops), you may get lucky and find that your favorite author will be in your event city on the day before or after your event, or you can schedule your event around their travel schedule.

→ **Book multiple dates as part of the same contract.** If you're holding a multi-city event series, and book the same speaker for all your dates, that speaker may negotiate a lower rate for each session.

What will likely not work: asking for a lower fee in exchange for a shorter program. Have you heard the expression, "I'd have written a shorter letter, but I didn't have the time"? In the paid speaking realm, *short does not equate with less valuable.* Many speakers will in fact need to spend *more* time customizing a shorter talk, so a fee reduction is almost always unappealing.

What About Booking a Free Speaker?

Naturally, as the longtime owner of a speakers' bureau, I'm going to have a bias against aiming to invite speakers at no cost. At the same time, I realize some groups cannot afford to pay the most buzzworthy presenters. So, if this is the route you intend to take, you should know the risks.

This is the most important reason I don't believe in free speakers: As they say, you often get what you pay for. The best speakers earn top dollar because they provide audiences with distinct points of view, fresh perspectives and rave-worthy inspiration. The ability to to develop and deliver tailored programs like this is the result of *years* of work, as well as hours of preparation to tailor remarks just for your event. Inviting a speaker or entertainer "on the cheap" when audiences expect—and deserve—the best experience can backfire.

Second, speakers coming in *pro bono* are inclined to sell or promote their products or services from stage (or less intrusively, in the "back of the room") to make up for the lack of a speaking fee. If you think your audience is down with this, go for it.

Finally, free speakers or entertainers have little "skin in the game." If they get a better offer, or have even a minor family emergency, they're much more likely to bail than if income and a strict cancellation clause are hanging in the balance.

A final note of caution: You should write a contract even for *pro-bono* performers. After all, this is a *business exchange* and each element of that exchange should be carefully spelled out to ensure the best possible outcome for everyone.

(For additional tips on presenters of all types, including how to navigate a speaker no show, see Chapter 13: How to Slay the Devil in the Details.)

 7.5 ## Even More Money-Saving Event Planning Ideas

Lastly, a few more non-obvious ways to save some moola:

→ **Join a gang.** If you're distributing any printed matter, you can probably save money by asking your printer about gang-run printing. Here, multiple printing projects (from multiple clients) are placed on a common paper sheet, so printing costs and paper waste are reduced. Also consider which elements of your signage recur across multiple events, and have these printed on, say, durable, reusable corrugated plastic.

→ **Tap the "Sharing Economy."** Ask your venue for contact information of other event planners holding meetings in or near your same space around the same time. Reach out to them to explore splitting expenses for professional speakers, performers, hosts, staging, tradeshow infrastructure, audio-visual equipment and décor/furniture.

→ **Get more social.** Which aspects of your paid advertising can migrate to no- or low-cost social media channels?

→ **Be un-swag-a-licious.** Swag bags, even when filled with no-cost sponsored items, still cost you something: time in finding sponsors, and then assembling, schlepping, storing and distributing the bags. After too many timesucks in this arena, we at TEDxSeattle decided we'd forego swag bags altogether and focus instead on giving attendees the gift of a one-of-a-kind, *experiential* event. In cultures overrun with *stuff*, this is often a welcomed change. If you've provided swag for years and then stop, be sure to communicate *why* you've decided to do so, and you'll inevitably ease the transition.

No matter what you're negotiating—whether cash payments or in-kind donations—get every single element in writing.

 **GET REAL:**

List three values your event stands for. Find three prospective sponsor companies that share these values. Then compose pitches to each one that speak to the needs of your prospective sponsors—keeping their needs and goals at the forefront. Uncover the right contact people, and send your proposals according to their fiscal calendars and submission timelines. Finally, follow up to ensure receipt and to inquire about next steps.

CHAPTER SUMMARY:
THREE THINGS TO REMEMBER

→ Successful sponsorship pitches speak first to each company's needs and goals. Then, once a sponsor is secured, integrate relevant messaging and moments that event-goers want to hear and experience. Don't interrupt attendees with what can only be perceived as annoying advertising.

→ Gain inspiration from a range of industries and event types as you procure and recognize sponsors; keep their needs top of mind, not (just) your need for support.

→ Securing a pro-bono or discounted speaker requires looking beyond the bottom-line cost, and broadening your awareness of what matters to the presenters.

CHAPTER 8

Unconventional Event Formats That Boost Engagement

There are almost as many event formats as there are events and infinite ways to mix and match programming to enliven otherwise dull agendas.

In this chapter, we'll explore some fabulous, non-obvious formats and games you can plug and play into all sorts of shindigs, for all sorts of audiences. As you read about them, think about how you can tweak certain elements to more fully align with your goals and make them even more impactful. All the while, stay curious: How can one of these ideas lead to the generation of other ideas?

Many of these formats can be rolled out at little or no cost; others require some budget. All are engaging.

Why Some Event Formats Work and Others Don't

Before we get to a list of formats and games to add more engagement to your events, let's examine what makes an event format successful in the first place. I believe it's these four features:

→ **Focused**: It zooms in and out of a few key take-aways instead of jumping between different topics.

→ **Flexible**: The approach caters to a range of skill levels, ages, audiences and topics.

→ **Functional**: The format may stand alone or be integrated into the larger event. (The twenty-minute TED-talk format is crazy popular because it can be inserted anywhere in an agenda. Or you can string together twenty-minute segments to form the entire gathering.)

→ **Fun**: People *want* to engage and participate, and the learning environment is relaxed to stimulate creativity.

With these "Four F's" in mind, let's dive into formats that engage attendees in innovative ways, starting with a creation of my own.

How to Use Mixing Chamber®

Mixing Chamber is a powerful format for generating original, actionable ideas while elevating participants' presentation skills. I designed it for No More Boring Meetings to resemble a TED-style event through which you curate, communicate and activate a group's best ideas to drive innovation and revenue.

Here's how it works:

First, we identify five to ten top thinkers and doers within a company, nonprofit or association, and help them hone their best ideas into short, engaging talks. Second, professional trainers steeped in the TED-talk model coach them in scripting and delivery skills. Then these "ready-for-prime-time" speakers present their short talks in front of a live audience of the organization's choosing.

The results? The clear way in which the participants have learned to communicate their ideas generates further ideation, innovation and even new products and services. What's more, these new thought leaders are now capable of presenting ideas and goals that will effectively distinguish the organization from its competition.

One benefit of using a Mixing Chamber is that you can transform your event from a cost center to a profit center.

Here's how: Invite top business associates or trade show vendors to join your event. Charge them a fee to get the Mixing Chamber-style presentation skills training so that they learn to deliver their subject-matter expertise in a fresh, audience-centered, short-talk format. Then, showcase their talks in an event structured around their compelling, idea-rich, TED-style talks for a paying audience.

8.3 Seventeen Ideas for Boosting Engagement

In this section, you will read several ideas for formats and techniques to boost engagement.

Idea 1 **Cricking**

Think of a historical figure(s) and/or celebrity(ies), alive or dead. Then consider: how would, say, Oprah approach this problem? What's Mark Zuckerberg's POV? What would Einstein bring to the equation? With this easy-to-implement, no-cost, surprisingly powerful format, attendees will generate great ideas in uncommon and delightful ways. And with the spotlight more on the well-known figure's brain, participants move beyond their own well-worn ways of looking at problems and view them from entirely new perspectives. For example, I once asked workshop attendees to assume the perspective of Ellen DeGeneres, and imagine that Ellen herself was helping to plan an event. "Ellen's" suggestions? Incorporate dancing; use honest, diplomatic and respectful communication; and ensure attendees participate purposefully.

Idea 2 **The currency of great ideas**

Good ideas can always be turned into currency. Here's a straightforward way to amplify idea generation via gamification. You'll also incent brilliance, create more engagement and boost learning—all for a few pennies or dollars per person, and for any sized gathering—from small team huddles to large conventions. Give each participant some form of fake currency that they can use *at their discretion* to award fellow attendees for their novel ideas or contributions throughout the event. The currency can be as basic and low-cost as chocolate coins or low-value gift cards. As the gathering ends, award the person with the most currency—and thereby the best ideas!—with a round of applause or a more substantial prize.

Idea 3 **The one-minute rebuttal**

Shake up people's thinking, inspire more interactivity and create a healthy debate with a set of one-minute rebuttals. Before a speaker presents from stage, tell attendees that they'll have the opportunity afterwards to come to the mic to share a sixty-second clip of their personal input on that presenter's talk. It could be a differing point of view, a follow-up example or even a full-on disagreement. Attendees will have the chance to experience both the "sage on the stage" (the main presenter) and the "guide on the side" (the attendee-turned-participant who has an also-valuable point of view). As the organizer, you'll want to stay true to the one-minute rule, and limit the number of rebuttals to a handful per speaker.

Idea 4 **Sung heroes**

We have all lamented the sad, unsung hero. Imagine the impact of having a professional song writer (or a super-creative member of your internal team) compose a short piece that honors top performers who don't usually get the spotlight with a custom, immortalizing song, and perform it live at your event.

Idea 5 **Walk and talk**

Simple, easy, fun. Get everyone out of their chairs and walking around in pairs or small groups to discuss specific applications of a meeting's content. Walking restores rather than depletes energy, moves ideas from short- to long-term memory and keeps brains engaged in the topics at hand. It also makes networking as simple as taking a stroll. (For more on the science of engagement, see Chapter 3: How to Transform Attendees into Participants.)

Idea 6 **Sixty ideas in sixty minutes**

Banish boredom with this fast-moving session. First, choose a subject of great interest to your audience— and a trained facilitator. Get a stop watch and a bell. Then invite your best experts onstage (whether outside speakers, SMEs, customers—or a mix). Ready, Set, GO: Each expert has just one minute to provide a tip or idea that fits within the over-arching content theme. Then, bing! Move to the next panelist until sixty minutes are up. Everyone gets practical strategies on relevant topics.

The Sixty Ideas format belongs in your back pocket for when a speaker cancels at the last minute.

(For non-obvious ways to manage a speaker no show, see Chapter 13: How to Slay the Devil in the Details.)

Idea 7 **Read best sellers—and foster better sellers!**

Let's say you hire a well-known author for a sales kickoff. You can boost sales, inspiration, team cohesion and actionable takeaways over time by starting a book club featuring that speaker's book. If your presenter has also given a TED or TEDx Talk, integrate that footage into the book discussion, too (and be sure to first check for any applicable licensing fees at TED.com).

Idea 8 **Surprise**

It may surprise you to see the word surprise listed as an "event format." I believe that this element is one of the most under-utilized and powerful event tools. Whether you surprise your audience with an unexpected guest, free autographed books or randomly given gift cards, be sure to keep a range of unknowns in your back pocket to add intrigue, buzz and vivid memories to any event. Need more reasons?

Surprise is proven to intensify our emotional experiences and boost the recall of these experiences.

Note, too, that unexpected event elements don't have to add to your budget; surprising attendees just means not revealing everything to them in advance.

Idea 9 **Strategic illustration**

Sometimes called graphic recording or graphic facilitation, this format features a professional artist who draws quick sketches illustrating the ideas being presented by speakers in real-time. The result? A visually engaging, re-usable illustration of one presentation or of an entire event. What's more, it makes for great social media content.

Idea 10 *Gamestorming*

Developed by designers, creators and authors Dave Gray, Sunni Brown and James Macanufo, Gamestorming is a toolkit of eighty games, diagrams and visual-thinking methods to help teams solve problems faster, create new products, communicate more effectively, identify an issue's root cause and find paths toward solutions. Some describe it as the low tech behind the high tech of Silicon Valley, and a key means by which product developers at top tech companies interact, innovate and iterate. Using paper, markers, sticky notes and more, Gamestormers solve problems such as lessening coffee cup waste and envisioning the next iPhone.

Idea 11 **Regiception**

Event goers typically use receptions to connect with those they already know. Foster higher energy and easy networking with a "Regiception"—a mash-up of your registration and opening reception at which attendees mingle *and* register to experience something truly new. Include food, drink and a variety of themed activities like throwback board games so that multi-generations can play with and learn from each other.

In developing and producing unique event formats, Jim Gilmore, speaker, event designer and co-author of the seminal book *The Experience Economy*, draws from a rich mix of footprints and techniques. The remaining event formats originate from his work, starting with "Regiception."[15]

Idea 12 **Lunch of one**

Have a smaller group? Provide physical and mental nourishment with a "lunch of one" and some unexpected quiet time. Each diner receives an envelope noting their meal location. The catch? You've booked a local restaurant for a table-for-one, *alone*. Each participant is asked to spend time over lunch recording what they learned so far at the event. Upon re-uniting, they share key learnings with the group. Note that "lunch of one" is a superb way to build in more repetition, reflection and white space as discussed in Chapter 2: How We Learn.).

Idea 13 **Field of teams**

Whether your audience is gathered on a field, in a ballroom or in an otherwise-stale tradeshow floor, establish stations at which participants can have a distinct experience. Make it something practical such as talking to a tech expert, or something seemingly frivolous but fun, like writing a note to be sent off in a helium balloon.

Idea 14 **PowerPoint improv**

Have attendees bring a favorite image-rich slide presentation on a flash drive. Place all drives into a bowl, and have participants grab a drive. After reviewing its contents, each participant must make a presentation based on slides they've never previously seen. It's an entertaining solution when you want a participant-led experience that builds think-on-your-feet skills.

Idea 15 **Power of narrow thinking**

Don't curse your long, narrow room. Instead, set up chairs in a way that resembles the inside of a plane fuselage. Issue boarding passes as name badges. Serve food and beverage on rolling carts down a middle aisle. Content = flight instruction!

Idea 16 **Meeting outside the box**

Use spaces that are not typically rented out for daytime events such as a rooftop, a revolving restaurant, a judo studio or a night club—at *noon*. Ask venues about useable space that's never been used. Your event venue becomes a focused, flexible, functional and fun format all of its own.

Idea 17 **No- and low-tech games**

Games are always a popular and engaging event format. Here are just a few low- or no-tech games that can be played with nothing more than a group of people, or via a robust, well-designed PowerPoint-, Prezi- or Keynote-style deck. Add cool graphics and sound effects for an even more memorable, multi-sensory experience.

→ **Improvisation** wraps teambuilding, listening and communication skills into one, no-tech, exceptionally fun package. All you need are people and a few improv game concepts. For ideas, check out the classic book, *Impro,* by Keith Johnstone.

→ **Fact or Crap:** Test the audience on company trivia and product details with this easy-to-design, true/false, slide-based game.

→ **Interactive idea wall.** Your event's ideas will come alive on a large wall on which participants share input over the course of an event. Poster boards, white boards on wheels or butcher paper all work well here. Be sure to take photos of your walls for both posting to social media and longer-term idea activation.

 GET REAL:

In this rubber-hits-the-road "get-real" segment, choose an event format such as Cricking, the Currency of Great Ideas, One-Minute Rebuttal, Walk-and-Talk or Surprise and try it at your next small team meeting to see how it impacts engagement. Or create your own format inspired by this chapter!

CHAPTER SUMMARY:
THREE THINGS TO REMEMBER

→ The most memorable event formats are focused, flexible, functional and fun.

→ The element of surprise is proven to intensify emotional experiences and boost the recall of these experiences.

→ Strategically chosen, non-obvious event formats inspired by ideas in this chapter will greatly elevate your event from status quo to kick-ass.

CHAPTER 9

How to Effectively Use Humor and Infotainment

Humor is the Swiss army knife of event tools. It boosts learning, attention, trust, energy, adaptability, memory, collaboration, optimism, circulation and lifespan. It lessens fear, stress and resistance to change. And it helps build safer, more inclusive and authentic communities.

Think I'm joking? Ask the researchers. Ask successful event planners who make a habit of incorporating humor into their events. Or just read on.

In this context, "humor" refers to thoughtful, strategic content that engages audiences on an emotional level and makes them laugh because it surprises and delights—in relevant (ROAR-ing!), contextual ways. It's not on par with comedic joke-telling, which is pure entertainment with no take-away value.

Brian Walter, who produces custom sketches that deliver information entertainingly, puts it this way:

"This isn't humor for humor's sake. It's humor as the servant of the message."

Used strategically, humor underscores authenticity, verve and memorability. When you carefully craft your message to align with your brand and personality, and use wit—not at the *expense* of getting attention, but as a *vehicle* for it—you gain a competitive *advantage*. You're different in a positive way.

Indeed, well-placed humor's ability to improve events is no laughing matter.

As a manager of countless events over my career, I consider humor the Holy Grail of engagement tools, because it alerts our minds as it lowers our defenses.

How often have you laughed with your arms crossed?!

Humor captures the attention of people who are otherwise bored and inattentive, and helps us be more creative, take more risks and forge ideal spaces for learning, trust building and collaboration. And when participants' brains are open, they absorb and retain more information.

We know events can be heavy, laborious and yes, boring. Pulling off a superb soiree is seriously hard work. Yet problem-solving is a bigger problem when our bodies and brains are under stress.

Inject levity into your event, and—no kidding!—you add critical mental breaks, catalyze creativity and generate new thinking. Humor also lowers stress in part because it releases "feel-good" dopamine and builds connection, collaboration and community.

9.1 When Humor Works—And When It Doesn't

When planners decide to omit humor from events, it's often with the belief that levity has no place in their organizations. But you'd be hard pressed to find an industry more serious than death and dying.

As vice president of professional development for the National Hospice and Palliative Care Organization, Barbara Bouton views humor as crucial to engaging her audiences of hospice and palliative care professionals. End-of-life care, by nature, is emotionally challenging. Burnout and compassion fatigue are common. Stress can be high.

While it may seem obvious at first, humor is indeed potent and appropriate medicine for those in industries often perceived as dark and joyless. Laughter reminds caregivers of their humanity, lowers stress, lessens their fears and that of the patients and helps everyone feel safer and more connected.

Bouton explains how they intentionally insert humorous content into their event programming, especially to close: "People have been listening to heavy sessions all week. Ending on lighter, funnier notes ensures they return home inspired and encouraged. Humor engages their heads and hearts, and leaves them feeling buoyant." Humorists' segments, adds Bouton with a smile, are consistently the highest-rated segments of her conferences.[16]

So when doesn't humor work?

Think relevancy and respect. If a laugh line isn't connected to the topic at hand, disses anyone in the audience or doesn't further your goals and messaging, then don't use it. When your intent is poignancy or pathos, steer clear of humor, too.

Remember, we're are not aiming for a string of comedic one liners. Rather, we're injecting moments of laughter that serve your big-picture event goals in strategic ways.

9.2 Information Delivered Entertainingly, AKA Infotainment

My No More Boring Meetings clients enjoy a wide range scalable, customized, humorous acts like song parodies that replace well-known lyrics with phrases specific to the event or organization. This is what we collectively call infotainment—information delivered entertainingly. Every word is about the people, the organization and the event messaging.

Take, for example, an insurance company challenged by a lack of cross-departmental communication. Consider some well-known John Denver song lyrics as a foundation: "You fill up my senses / like a night in a forest." Add a singer dressed to look like Denver (round glasses, lots of denim). Live on stage, he croons a lyrical parody, "You fill up my budget / with some make-believe numbers..."

Another: In corporate events, the C-Suite is often removed from the employee base. A humor-driven solution? Matching Celeb, where the audience is shown a photo of one of their actual senior leaders on screen before the host reveals another photo of an actual celebrity who closely resembles the leader. Each example is funnier than the last. Audiences—and the execs—love the experience because it's fast, funny and customized, and achieves a serious feat of powerfully humanizing leaders in unexpected ways.

And then there's the twist on TV's Dr. Phil McGraw who worked with the guests on his show, Dr. Phil, to achieve behavioral breakthroughs or to overcome limits in their thinking. Taking Dr. Phil's cue into the event world, infotainer Brian Walter (already sporting his own bald head, plus a Dr. Phil-like fake mustache) has been known to show up to host a custom "Dr. Fill" segment. Impersonating the real Dr. Phil's direct and folksy style, Dr. Fill surfaces and then crushes real and perceived challenges the audience has with a key issue, such as managing the intricacies of bank compliance.

In each case—song parody, Matching Celeb, and Dr. Fill—every element is carefully researched, and clients are able to review and edit drafts in advance, so they can feel completely confident in the scripts before show time. We also ensure the sketches are within the legal bounds of parody.

The power of infotainment is multi-fold.

Gameshows create learning opportunities, and offer un-boring, engaging ways to educate and discover what audiences know and don't know. Custom-written songs and videos about products, customers, audiences, objectives and accomplishments create shared experiences, and can also address uncomfortable truths, bust myths and humanize leaders through humor.

(For more examples of infotainment, see Chapter 8: Unconventional Event Formats.)

9.3 What Are Some Reliable Sources of Humor?

Aside from infotainment, what are some additional sources of humor that can engage event audiences and generate that all-important Return On Attendee Relevance (ROAR)?

Inviting a stand-up comedian is, ahem, an obvious choice for interjecting humor. What about some more non-obvious sources of The Funny?

→ **A well-chosen host** is a superb, efficient way to outsource the creation and delivery of humor— and be confident in the result. Your audience will be grateful that you chose a masters of ceremonies with a proven track record for injecting thoughtful, improvisational remarks. (For more tips, see Chapter 6: How to Use Panels, Q&A Sessions and Event Hosts.)

→ **At TEDxSeattle**, we often align our speakers' content and event themes in humorous ways that engages attendees, with support from Interplay Experience Design (a Seattle-based company that builds participatory experiences aligned with learning objectives). For example, after a talk that debated whether Big Foot is real, a large person dressed as Sasquatch roamed the halls. Strolling astronauts appeared in alignment with another event's space theme.

→ **Turn your quest for more humor into a profit center** by commissioning your sponsors to produce short, funny videos that showcase their products in comical, yet message-rich ways. Then, play these videos as interstitial breaks in between heavier, more serious content. This becomes a profit center when you have sponsors pay for the opportunity to get their brands in front of your audience.

 GET REAL:

Watch a favorite sitcom or late-night show. And this time—*wink, wink, nudge, nudge*—watch it differently. Pay close attention to the comedic devices employed and consider what makes them effective. Then, use your new insights to help determine where you can employ similar structures to enchant audiences at your event.

CHAPTER SUMMARY:
THREE THINGS TO REMEMBER

→ Humor is the Holy Grail of engagement tools because it boosts learning, attention, trust, energy, adaptability, memory, collaboration, optimism, circulation and lifespan; lessens fear, stress and resistance to change; and helps build safer, more inclusive and authentic communities.

→ Irrelevant and disrespectful humor never works—and when your intent is poignancy or pathos, avoid humor, too.

→ Well-suited sources of event humor include infotainment; a professional humorist; roaming, costumed characters; and curated, on-theme videos (which can also generate revenue).

CHAPTER 10

How to Think Like a TED Conference Organizer

Let's say it takes you about thirty seconds to read this paragraph. In that time, about 1,000 people worldwide have started to watch a TED Talk online. That's about thirty per second. Egads! What is it about the TED brand that makes their talks and events so compelling to so many across the globe? What has the hundreds who attend "Big TED" in Vancouver, British Columbia every year vying for a limited number of expensive seats at a nearly week-long, industry-agnostic conference?

As an attendee at global TED events and a longtime TEDxSeattle volunteer, I'll share what I think makes TED so remarkable.

My purpose here isn't only to take you behind the scenes of this conference experience.

What draws billions of people to both live and recorded TED and TEDx Talks is, in fact, achievable by all event planners.

Most event planners simply ask: What should we do at this event? Where should we hold it? Whom should we invite?

TED sees the possibilities inherent in gathering people together through an entirely different lens, and asks: What are the most pressing, compelling ideas in the world right now? Who is most suited to talk about them? What can we do that's never been done before to engage the world in these ideas? How can we re-pattern the future?

And in this chapter, I ask: How can non-TED event organizers design conferences that are worthy vehicles for sharing truly fresh ideas that impact the future—and the organization?

Seven Lessons That TED Teaches Us

We can start by applying these seven non-obvious lessons, which I discovered through my impassioned love affair with TED, and which all start (conveniently) with the letter C.

Lesson 1 **Content that's viral worthy**

TED's raison dêtre is to offer the world "ideas worth spreading." It's a global lab of sorts that seeks to push the world's boundaries. Similarly, at TEDxSeattle, we aim to "crack our audiences' heads open" with fresh, compelling ideas.

Let's look at the foundational building blocks that make ideas spread widely in the first place. I believe the ingredients of a viral TED Talk are many: a story-driven hook that's easy to recall. A counter-intuitive, surprising or even controversial concept that creates connection, curiosity and empathy between a speaker and a listener. A story arc that focuses on one idea (not three, not five). All offered in readily accessible, bite-sized, sharable forms (video, podcasts, radio, social media).

To actually generate such viral-worthy content, TED and TEDx teams ask: What are the top ideas worth spreading at this event, in alignment with our chosen theme? And then they curate prospective speakers who can deliver on those ideas, by asking them: Why this idea, why you and why now?

It is a high bar, yet in a world where we're all distracted and overwhelmed, our events must provide intellectually compelling and quickly actionable content.

Let's look at two examples of ideas that began as thoughts in people's minds—and then, via TED, went globally viral.

Simon Sinek (who was unknown when he delivered his "Start with Why" talk at TEDxPuget Sound in 2009) showed that the most successful leaders and companies do something very different than the rest of us. They have a compelling why for what they do. They communicate this why from the inside out. And customers buy not what they do, but why they do it.

Then there's Dr. Brene Brown. Her one idea? That there is power in vulnerability. She delivered this idea on the TEDxHouston stage with vulnerability—and humor.

Sinek and Brown are now both celebrated speakers thanks to their distinct, fresh, counter-intuitive, curiosity-driving, easy-to-remember ideas: Sinek's "Start with Why," and Brown's "There's Power in Vulnerability." Their TED Talks are now among the most watched in history (in the forty-million-views-apiece range at press time) and they've gone on to become globally known thought leaders.

To further explore how to turn an idea into a talk, or into other forms of thought leadership, I recommend http://storiedthoughts.com.

Lesson 2 **Compulsively concise**

But having a great idea is just the beginning. The most viral-worthy TED and TEDx speakers—in addition to their great ideas—are willing to be coached through plenty of script writing and rewriting and yet more rewriting. All in an effort to be compulsively concise.

A core TED principle: Make it great; keep it short. AKA "less is more." Generally, the maximum length of a TED Talk is eighteen minutes (and getting shorter). Why eighteen and not, say, fifteen or twenty? Research shows that eighteen is long enough to make a specific point and tell a good story, but not long enough to bore people to death. Before TED hit the scene, you rarely saw events with talks this short. But now we know that being compulsively concise makes for extremely compelling programming.

Please understand, though, if you seek to bring a TED-like feel to your events, a talk need not be exactly eighteen minutes. Some of the best ideas can be expressed in an extremely short time. Three minutes was all one TED speaker needed to show a better way to tie our shoe laces. It's garnered two million+ views—and counting.

Delivering a short, effective talk takes discipline and practice.

Lisa Phelps Dawes, a four-time Emmy award-winning writer and director, co-chair of the TEDxSeattle speaker team and founder of a thought leadership consultancy, describes the process of refining a talk to its essence this way: "Through deliberate practice, a speaker becomes clearer in her thoughts, and she becomes more grounded. She feels more connected to what she's saying because she's sharpened her thinking to the point of conviction. Every word aligns with her beliefs, intention and desire to share her idea with the audience."

Lisa also notes that, "Honing drafts for a talk is about challenging the idea and how it's expressed, line by line: 'Is this what I mean? Is it clear? Is it what the audience needs to hear right now to understand?' You're always writing with the audience in mind."

Want to know how long a talk will be when spoken live, based on a script's word count? Try this handy calculator: http://storiedthoughts.com/free-speech-calculator/

Lesson 3 **Curated speakers, audiences and sponsors**

The entire TED experience is curated. The word curate comes from the Latin, meaning "to take care."

In the context of a TED conference, effective speaker, audience and partner curation consists of intentional, thoughtful framing of topics around a central theme.

TED and many TEDx audiences are also curated—that is, hand selected. Everyone who registers to attend a global TED event must apply to attend, and not all are accepted. This rigorous audience curation process helps ensure a broad and unusual range of viewpoints, cultures, ages and professions in the delegate base—and thereby creates greater demand for an intentionally limited number of seats.

In addition, TED is selective about the brands and organizations that they work with as sponsors, so ultimately, the entire event experience is exclusive and truly one of a kind.

Beyond gaining quality content and experiences through curation, you also:

→ **Gain more control** over the vibe, design and mix of experiences and the mix of participants.

→ **Bake in a more exclusive feel** to events, which leads to more demand, which means you can generally charge higher registration fees.

→ **Save time and eliminate stress** because you're less likely to be caught in analysis paralysis; you're less likely to have (too?) many competing visions vying for attention. A small group, or a single person, determines the vision behind the event, and how that vision is going to be achieved.

Lesson 4 **Compelling conversations that lead to synchronicity**

Surely, when you combine a carefully curated speaker lineup, and place them before a hand-selected audience, you've got a recipe for fascinating dialog. But let's look for a moment at the non-obvious. On a deeper level are "invisible" conversations unfolding too between speakers and attendees. Everyone's brain waves, heart beats and breathing patterns are synching up and aligning as ideas are shared, and as audiences listen to and learn from speakers. A synchronistic hive mind of human connection is formed.

Lesson 5 **Community and conductivity for continually connected global learners**

The chance to mingle with, learn from and network among superbly interesting people from scores of countries, all at once, is the main reason I have spent years playing in the TED and TEDx sandbox.

At just one such event, I met an experimental anthropologist, a social concierge, an inventor of space equipment and a cruciverbalist—and that's just for starters. We talked about peace. The lack of peace. Nanotechnology. Fireflies. **We laughed. Cried. Got TED-aches. Snowshoed. Head-scratched. Ziplined. Raised glasses in late-night toasts. Not one boring conversation in five days!**

By "continually connected," I am referring to the TEDConnect App to which all conference goers gain access. Since the app stays active after the event, we can still connect with fellow TEDActive and TEDSummit attendees years later. When traveling, I can likely find a fellow TEDster who is willing to meet up, no matter where I go.

While the T in TED stands for technology, sometimes a simpler solution is called for. Conductivity and idea-sharing at TED events often happens on large, modular walls where we post questions, ideas and attendee-organized activities. This simple, low-tech approach to boosting engagement connects people in a more interactive community. And these low-tech modalities don't require that attendees always have their smart phones (AKA "weapons of mass distraction") in hand to connect and communicate.

So...how can you grant this level of deep, continual access to your attendees, no matter your industry, demographic or budget?

Lesson 6 **Coaching, on steroids**

Most TED and some TEDx speakers receive extensive content, scripting and delivery coaching by seasoned instructors.

Head of TED Chris Anderson counsels TED Talkers with this advice: "Your number-one mission as a speaker is to take something that matters deeply to you and to rebuild it inside the minds of your listeners. We'll call that something an idea. A mental construct that they can hold on to, walk away with, value, and in some ways be changed by."[17] (To hear more from Anderson on how to think of an idea: https://www.youtube.com/watch?v=-FOCpMAww28)

Further, another fundamental principle of TED-style talks is that a TED coach is always sure to ask the speaker the following: What purpose or idea is the TED Talk serving? And it can't be in service of the speaker! Rather, the talk must serve and support the idea.

Then, after what are often dozens of hours scripting, presentation coaching and rehearsals, speakers are ready to deliver their ideas worth spreading to actual audiences.

And why do billions tune in? TED Talks capture our imagination because they offer fresh, never-before-seen insights that ignite curiosity, help us navigate the world and shape the future. That three-minute shoe-lace-tying talk mentioned above? Its "higher purpose" idea is that small changes can yield big results.

Want to tap this kind of coaching support for your speakers? No More Boring Meetings offers TED-style coaching in live and virtual settings.

Lesson 7 **Choice**

TED attendees don't choose from breakout sessions. They all watch the same talks in a general-session format, which also serves to more readily catalyze that "synchronistic hive mind" mentioned above in Lesson

4. But they do get a great deal of choice during the rest of the event. I saw this first hand at TEDActive, which is one of TED's events for "global innovators." TEDActive ran in parallel to the main TED conference, and as TEDActivators, we watched the TED Talks in Whistler, British Columbia as they were simulcast from Vancouver.

For example, we had choices at every phase of the agenda. We were given alternative forms of interaction—with others, with our own thoughts, with content, with new ideas. We could eat anywhere in the venue and got to choose where we watched the simulcasted talks. There were at least a half a dozen types of seats, including bean bags and sofas, in the main simulcast room. Another viewing room, the lounge, offered a screen on the ceiling with a bed underneath. (You can imagine how popular this spot was!)

We even got to choose the "personality" of the floor we stayed on at the venue hotel. Are you a stay-up-late-and-be-boisterous type? There was a floor just for your tribe. Would you like quiet contemplation? There was another wing for you. It was a rare and wonderful offering, and one that I hope becomes more prevalent for event goers. Why don't you try it?

As a devoted TEDster, I can say with conviction that the world needs more "TED-ifying," i.e. more of what this brand brings to the world: fresh, compelling ideas shared in a community filled with authentic, human connections. A worldwide campfire of possibilities and revolutionary solutions stoked by the flames of knowledge.

How ideal, then, that we event professionals are in the perfect industry to achieve just that.

To close out this section, let's look back at this list of qualities and elements that constitute TED conference design:

1. **Content that's viral worthy.**

2. **Compulsively concise.**

3. **Curated speakers, audiences and sponsors.**

4. **Compelling conversations that lead to synchronicity.**

5. **Community of continually connected global learners.**

6. **Coaching speakers to give the talks of their lives.**

7. **Choice, and lots of it.**

GET REAL:

With this background on the what and why of curation, take a moment and consider what *you* can curate. What about a series of event venue tours that isn't available anywhere else? A group of SMEs never before assembled? A never-to-be-seen-again set of auction items for your fundraiser?

Or, what other element from the above list will you integrate into your next event to stage an experience that's as viral worthy as a popular TED Talk? (It's your choice on whether it also starts with C;)

READ THE FULL STORY:

Go behind the scenes to see how TEDxSeattle curates audience engagement experiences for sponsors.

CHAPTER SUMMARY:
THREE THINGS TO REMEMBER

→ TED is a global force that engages about 1,000 people worldwide every thirty seconds in videos featuring "ideas worth spreading," proving it has plenty to teach us about producing more compelling events.

→ Its secret sauce—available to event organizers who up their game—consists of concise, viral-worthy content delivered by carefully curated, coached speakers...combined with real-time conversations in a choice-rich community of learners.

→ A core TED principle is: to make it great, keep it short. AKA "less is more." This requires meticulously scripting and honing remarks so that speakers' thinking is sharper, and audiences are more engaged.

CHAPTER 11

How to Produce and Stage Manage an Event Like a Pro

Under an event's bright lights, see-all cameras and unforgiving image magnification, missteps can become amplified. Yet most of them can be prevented with some non-obvious approaches.

Slides figure prominently in most events these days. After all, PowerPoint, Prezi and Keynote software all make it so dang easy to create decks of all sorts. But some of the most powerful talks—gasp!—are slide-free.

Martin Luther King, Jr. didn't have one. Neither did Winston Churchill. Elizabeth Gilbert, in her two exceptionally popular TED Talks, went without.

Three revolutionary presenters, and not one slide.

These days, we tend to believe that for event messaging and programming to sink in, speakers must rely on visually rich slides on big screens.

Well-designed slides can augment ideas. They can inform and sway audiences. And they can even change the world. (Consider Al Gore's slide-dependent "An Inconvenient Truth" talk). At the same time, there's a valid argument for slides getting in the way of learning.

Much of the research proves that large, projected visuals make it much *harder* for audiences to manage their cognitive load. In other words, we humans—despite are deepest desires—cannot multitask.

The Upside of Killing Your Slides

Depending on the content and context, both listening to a speaker and trying to take in the information on their slide deck is rarely possible. At best, we can devote a mediocre level of cognitive awareness—sometimes referred to as continual partial attention—to what we see and hear.

Need more proof? Brain science offers presenters cutting-edge insights on how the brain facilitates learning and memory.

A study in the journal *Nature Neuroscience* found significant differences in brain activity in active vs. passive learners. Specifically, active learners who have some control over their learning environments and have agency over how information is absorbed, significantly enhanced their ability to remember it. When learning actively, larger parts of the brain turn on and "get functionally connected when you're actively exploring the world."[18] (For tools to help event goers become active participants, see Chapter 3: How to Transform Attendees into Participants.)

How to Make Presentations Compelling (Without Using Slides)

Imagine your keynoter is about present and—gasp!—the power goes out. What will she do to convey the most important points? A great way to apply this unlikely situation to real life: Re-design a presentation with a literal "lights-out" scenario in mind to inspire new thinking.

Since the lights *will* most certainly stay on at your event (!), what can presenters do—without relying on slides—to boost memorability and takeaway?

→ A well-told story often trumps any slide when it comes to what the human brain will remember

→ Short videos

→ Graphic illustration (invite someone to draw out your ideas while you talk)

→ Interviews

→ A testimonial letter from a real customer

→ Quizzes and game shows with ties to pop culture. For example, create your own "Deal or No Deal" game to explore negotiation strategies, or play a company Jeopardy game to test audience knowledge about other departments.

→ A product demo

→ A (relevant) custom song about a topic, sung live from the stage

→ An exclusive "reveal"

→ Tightly timed roundtables that generate new ideas, bridge solutions or air frustrations, along with awards given for the best ideas as voted on by peers

→ Improv skits about next year's product line that get sales teams thinking fast on their feet

As you investigate different ways to present beyond slides, try brainstorming with something other than a digital device: a note pad, white board, sticky notes, napkin, chalk. You're more likely to venture beyond linear thinking into more creative realms and land on novel ideas.

 ## 11.3 Ten Tips to Produce Your Event Like a Pro

Whether your event ultimately features lots of slides, no slides or somewhere in between, the overall experience can be thought of as a theater production—no matter its size or scope. So, you need to set the stage.

So, without further ado, we present the "Late-Night-with-David-Letterman" style **Top 10 Ways to Produce Your Event Like a Total Pro:**

Tip 10 **Be slide savvy**

When you use slides, be sure to maximize the audience's ability to take in the information from the presenters' visuals. The industry standard for projection screen format (AKA aspect ratio; that is, the shape and proportion of slides as they appear on screen) is 16:9. (Many in healthcare and academia still run slides in 4:3.) Whichever you choose, communicate your ratio to all slide users so that they are all consistent. Also, consider insisting that all slides steer clear of predominantly white backgrounds. White is hard on the eyes and reveals hotspots in the projection.

DOWNLOAD: RESOURCE

Wondering what minimum font size to use on slides based on variables such as screen width? Visit https://www.thinkoutsidetheslide.com/ selecting-the-correct-font-size

Tip 9 **Perfect your projection**

Well-designed slides are only as good as the projectors that project them. So, don't assume your venue has the most well-suited projectors for what you want to achieve. If, for example, your event is in a theater, which is designed for live, slide-less performances, the in-house projector likely isn't ideal for large-scale slide and video projection. Check to be sure. And, no matter where your event, have a backup projector on hand in case the one provided blows. Cuz that would just blow.

Tip 8 **Shine a light**

A non-obvious tip about lighting: If those on the stage are under inadequate lighting, those in the seats are less likely to trust what they see and hear. You've spent untold resources on finding and preparing your presenters, so don't skimp on illuminating them when it's their time to shine in the spotlight! Then place markers on stage that give presenters boundaries to move within to remain in the light.

Tip 7 **Set up for success**

Let's say you tell the venue to set seven tables, each table seating ten people. If you don't tell them exactly where in the room you want the tables to be placed, you may need to move everything last minute to meet your needs. So, always give the venue a detailed diagram so that you avoid misunderstandings. If you don't, the staff will decide for you. Then always make sure to check that the seating is correct when you arrive.

Tip 6 **Lessen your load (in)**

Create a detailed production schedule and ensure that all production vendors (lighting, screens, projectors, furniture rental, staging, décor, centerpieces, catering, linens) have the chance to provide feedback on it. You want to make sure that they understand what the others have committed to, and when each will arrive, so load-in is smooth. Also, note the rehearsal time so that the AV team is ready to go when they are needed. Send a final copy and request written approval so you have "insurance" against any unwarranted cost overruns. For example, lights on the ceiling will need to be in place before the tables and chairs are set. Sound obvious? Tell that to the production team that had to move tables out of the way to accommodate a Genie® lift so they could set up a spotlight last minute.

Tip 5 Hire professionals

If your budget allows, hire a show caller, AKA stage manager. This person communicates all show cues to your production team and coordinates the comings and goings of anyone who shows up on stage. Also, consider hiring a producer, who will coordinate all your AV equipment, pull together the show flow and communicate at an advanced level with the AV company. If your event is smaller, one person can fulfill the role of show caller and producer.

Tip 4 Rehearse in advance of rehearsal

Great events become so because all the "players in the show" meet to review every detail. To do so, schedule a pre-con ("pre-conference," or sometimes called a "logistics all-up") one to two weeks before your event with your event team, along with a representative from the event venue and all the actual production partners who will be present at the event, to review the production schedule and the run of show. (The ROS is a detailed, timed sequence of what will unfold at your event, and who's responsible for each aspect. Also called a rundown or show flow.) Catering, registration check in, room use, signage and your event script are all reviewed (and adjusted) during a pre-con. (See Chapter 12: How to Plan an Event on (Almost) Any Timeline for more details on these production meetings.)

Tip 3 **Gather your posse's phone numbers**

This is a critical and non-obvious step: Make sure to have the cell phone numbers of every single person involved with your shindig. That means decision makers, staff, production crew, speakers, hosts and venue representatives. Add corresponding hotel room numbers while you're at it. When you need to reach someone quickly, you'll be glad you took this step.

Tip 2 **Test, test, re-test**

The day of, make sure all your media—music, voice of God, slides, amplifiers, confidence monitors, teleprompter, props, screens, lighting, microphones (always use fresh batteries!), special effects, rigging, videos (check both the sound and projected image)—are working. Test and re-test again. Then ensure you and the AV team have a backup plan for every component, in case of total failure.

And the #1 Tip for Producing Your Event Like a Total Pro...

Tip 1 **Rehearse**

This is actually very non-obvious, says corporate event production veteran of twenty-five years, Cynthia Bishop. She believes the failure to rehearse is the #1 mistake event organizers make. Yet every show needs a rehearsal—you just don't want your first one to happen in front of a live audience! Ideally, your rehearsal has everyone reviewing the entire show in real time, and making adjustments along the way.

Plan to allot twice as much time for a rehearsal as the live event (i.e. if the event is four hours long, rehearsal will likely take eight hours as you'll need added time to make and communicate adjustments). You're aiming for smooth transitions throughout, with no awkward "dead-air" time. Some execs, speakers and performers may insist they don't need to rehearse. Your retort?

The rehearsal isn't as much for those on stage as it is for everyone backstage. In a well-run rehearsal, you're going through every programming element: walk-on music, slide advancement, thorough equipment testing, lighting cues, video and audio run-throughs; every cue and transition, every intro and outro. You're looking for gaps and glitches—in advance—so they can be corrected and don't happen at show time!

 GET REAL:

Next time you attend an event that features slides, take note of other ways the information in the slides could have been communicated. Then apply these insights to your upcoming gathering.

CHAPTER SUMMARY:
THREE THINGS TO REMEMBER

Slide decks do not guarantee more attentive audiences; in fact, some believe slides distract more than they engage.

In lieu of slides, try videos, graphic illustration, games, product demos, roundtables and improvisation.

Deck or no deck, your event—to kick ass—must be professionally produced, so up your game on projection, lighting, load ins, communication and most of all, a full run through, because the #1 mistake event organizers make is to skimp on rehearsals.

CHAPTER 12

How to Plan an Event on (Almost) Any Timeline

I've found that one of the best things about an event is that, come hell or high water, it's going to happen. You're going to go into *labor*, and that "baby" is going to be born.

Let's dive into making this "labor-intensive," deadline-driven environment work in your favor—whether you have three years, three months or three days (!) to pull your gathering together.

Sometimes the best way to learn something is to learn how not to do something.

With decades of work in the events world, I often see people wasting time due to a lack of systems and strategy. If you don't just read this book—and actually *do and apply* its principles and processes—you'll inevitably save time. You'll work smarter and not harder. And generate the kind of kick-ass results you crave.

Four Common Timesucks (And How to Solve Them)

In planning events, most planners will encounter several common timesucks. Here are a few of them along with some ideas for how to solve them.

Timesuck: Failing to focus on defining your event's content and takeaways while busy speakers' schedules fill up.

Such an undisciplined lack of tactics will suck weeks out of your life and the spirit from your team.

Solution: Instead, ask and answer the four questions in Chapter 5: How to Curate a Kick-Ass Speaker Lineup to add focus to your thinking and smart action to your event content. This will allow you to develop a **Content**

Map to streamline your programming development in ways that keep everyone on task. The final result = exactly what matters most to event goers.

Timesuck: Failing to "repeat to remember."

This one may seem like a contradiction. Isn't repetition inherently a time suck? Nope, and here's why. If your participants are not given the chance to revisit and review content periodically throughout the event, they may as well have been absent from the event. Then all the preparation, education and expense were for naught. The most cutting-edge brain science proves that whether you're an event planner or an event goer, important takeaways must be repeated to be remembered—within two hours of the first exposure. Or we may just as well...forget it!

Solutions: Give participants time to review notes, play games and quizzes, or teach song lyrics that repeat key concepts.

Timesuck: Falling short of reaching your most important stakeholders' goals.

Unless you hold the highest position in the organization, you probably answer to someone. (Even if you're the top dog, you are probably beholden to stakeholders or sponsors). I see many event organizers waste time—often in the eleventh hour of an event-planning process—scrambling to satisfy a stakeholder's desires because they didn't take the time to clarify expectations and responsibilities from the beginning.

Solution: Avoid this stress and possible belly flop by asking your top stakeholders to define their most important objectives as soon as possible. Find out what these results-hungry "patrons of the party" want, so you can strategically decide how you will generate these results.

What if, for example, your event's success rides on the CEO's presentation, but the CEO doesn't realize that the video accompanying her speech (a video requiring two weeks of production time) cannot be prepared until her speech is written, and she's planning to have her remarks completed two *days* before the conference?

Maybe your nonprofit must abide by new federal guidelines for securing funding for the next fiscal year. Now, you need your attendee base to consist of at least 65% women and minorities, but your marketing team isn't aware of this new rule because it didn't ask the right questions.

Or perhaps an event goal is to ensure that a behind-the-scenes donor gets a front row seat during the celebrity's keynote. But you didn't invite him, and the event is tomorrow.

Solution: In each of these examples, had you sooner known about all stakeholders' critical dependencies and asked better questions, you would have saved time and saved face.

Timesuck: You're stuck.

Is your recurring event the same year after year? Is attendance flatlining and buzz dwindling? Then it's time to stop wasting time, retool and unstick yourself. **Before you roll out last year's agenda and just plug in new presenters, consider an entire re-vamp.** Your gatherings have lost their edge and no longer meet attendees' needs. Your value proposition may not be that valuable. Instead?

Solution: Re-focus your thinking. If you are really intent on expanding what's possible at your event, bring together a mix of your participants for a professionally facilitated focus group. You'll get more candid, thoughtful, insightful and actionable input from the attendees' point of view, and a much deeper dive on the event experience than you might from a simple survey.

Solution: Expand your event experience. "Get outta Dodge" and attend some events yourself to generate a renewed sense of what's possible. It'll be worth the investment. I've listed some highly innovative conference options in the Compelling Conferences to Check Out section at the end of this book.

Solution: Switch up the programming. Learn how by exploring ideas in this guide, especially from Chapter 5: How to Curate a Kick-Ass Speaker Lineup; Chapter 8: Unconventional Event Formats; Chapter 10: How to Think Like a TED Conference Organizer; Chapter 11: How to Produce and Stage Manage an Event Like a Pro; and Chapter 14: How to Take Smart Risks..

Solution: Try a new, nontraditional venue. What about a skyscraper rooftop? Coworking space? Vineyard? Museum? Music studio? Art gallery? Science lab?

GET REAL:

Uncover every event stakeholders' goals, and work backwards to ensure each need is addressed. Do so and you're the event hero; fail to do so, and you're in deep doo-doo.

 ## How to Track Your Meeting's Productivity Cost

What if you could calculate the productivity cost of taking people off their "regular work" and into meetings? One Fortune 500 company built a simple and powerful "meeting cost tracker" tool to do just that.

Here's how the tool works. You enter the number of attendees as well as an average labor burden rate, which is an employee's hourly rate plus the per-hour value of an employee's benefits. You also factor in meeting length.

Attendees x labor burden rate (in dollars) x hours in meeting = productivity cost

For easy math, let's go with fifty attendees, with an average labor burden rate of $100 per hour, who gather for two hours.

Post the tracker so it's visible to everyone. Start the meeting as you start the tracker. You'll see a calculation of what the meeting is costing—in real time down to the last cent.

So, in the above example, the cost to the company is $10,000 (50 x $100 x 2).

As they say, we don't argue with our own data. Now we must decide whether the accomplishments are worth that money—and productivity loss. If so, you scored! If not, you must decide how to streamline the guest list and the agenda in the future. Or, decide if there is a more succinct way to communicate what was discussed in person. Knowledge is power.

The company that built this tracker is just starting to roll it out. One manager, right out of the gate, found a way to save $40,000 in one month.

What would your meeting cost tracker reveal?

12.3 How to Create Your Comprehensive Event Plan

Before we lay out a detailed event timeline, allow me to suggest: If, as a new-to-this-game or "accidental" event organizer, you read through this timetable of to-dos with a sense of calm—an assured belief that "you've got this"—great!

If, rather, you review it with an increasing sense of "holy sh--," I respectfully suggest you hire a professional meeting planner to outsource some or all of the planning process. (If you want some stellar recommendations, let me know.)

After all, when we try something new, something as surprisingly complex as event planning, we almost never know what we don't know. In the wild world of events, changing one small element can have a substantial ripple effect.

An example: Let's say you decide, half way through planning, that rather than have a set menu, you'll give all attendees multiple entrée choices. This "small" change will generate a cascade of additional actions: You will need to augment the registration process so people can note their meal preference, create a system to track and manage guests' choices and communicate these to the caterer, come up with a way to deal with guests who, you find upon arrival, never noted a meal preference, or who thought they did, and indicate to servers what each guest has ordered. And that's just one small adjustment.

To help you plan for your event no matter how long you have, you will find two versions of a helpful event planning guide in the online resources for this book. You can use either as a checklist to ensure you are focused on all the right details and getting them done in a timely fashion to set your event up for success.

DOWNLOAD: RESOURCE

To access the "Whole Enchilada" four- to six-month+ timeline and the "Holy-Guacamole," in-a-pinch timeline, download them online.

 **GET REAL:**

What's YOUR #1 meeting time waster—and your solution?

 CHAPTER SUMMARY:
THREE THINGS TO REMEMBER

→ To save time and boost event impact, conduct a focus group and ask stakeholders to define their most important objectives early on in order to obtain the insight necessary to develop a Content Map to plan programming strategically and efficiently.

→ The meeting cost tracker—attendees x labor burden rate (in dollars) x hours in meeting = productivity cost—shows the exact cost of taking people off their "regular work" and into meetings.

→ Detailed event timelines included with this guide ensure nothing falls through the cracks.

CHAPTER 13

How to Slay the Devil in the Details

Much of this guide focuses on big-picture ideas and processes. When to hold a meeting, and when not to. How brains work, and how to remember more. Tools for thinking about content in fresh ways. Attention-grabbing strategies and risk taking.

But we all know that the devil's in the details. To ensure our events are truly best in class and kick ass, we must also be masters and mistresses of minutiae.

We need some non-obvious, easy-to-use lessons for managing all of those hundreds of details without giving ourselves a stress attack. This chapter will share lessons on how to manage the logistics of any event like a pro, including how to manage the situation when things (inevitably!) go wrong in unpredictable ways. (For more detailed, checklist-style timelines, see the online resources for this book.)

13.1 How to Manage the Details With Speakers

When it comes to booking speakers for your event and managing their logistics, there is plenty that can go awry. Here is a helpful list of tips for how to manage all the details that go into booking and working with speakers.

Tip 1 Submit thorough offers

When you're making offers to speakers and entertainers, do you ask for everything you need? A content conference call, media interview(s), a VIP reception, book signing, social media posts, post-event follow up? You'll maximize your investment in your speaking talent, avoid disappointment and save time when these points are covered in the offer. Better to over-ask than to forget a key request, as you will likely be out of luck if you inquire after the contract's been signed.

Tip 2 Practice speakers' intros

When people introducing presenters fumble or appear unprepared, not only do they look foolish, but they also create an irrevocable bad first impression of the speaker you've worked so hard to invite and prep. So, ask them to practice the intro. Yes, even if it's short, and especially if it's long. Provide phonetic spellings of every difficult word on the script. But never edit speakers' or entertainers' intros without their permission. These are carefully scripted for a reason, and if you change 'em, you may inadvertently distract presenters just as they walk on.

Tip 3 **Prevent disembodiment**

Are you using Image Magnification (IMAG) and/or are you videorecording what happens on stage for future use? Then be sure to ask speakers to wear clothing that contrasts with your stage backdrop so that they don't blend in (black clothing on black pipe and drape for example!). This way, your live and recorded footage won't feature people with disembodied heads.

Tip 4 **Avoid speaker no-shows**

Having a speaker not show up is definitely a "worst nightmare scenario," but there are a few professional methods to minimize the chances of this happening.

First, limit the impact of flight delays. When inviting an out-of-town speaker, include a clause in your agreements that requires presenters book flights with at least one back up or buffer flight after it, in case of cancellation or delay. This simple, uncommon step can save you and your speaker untold worry. You may also want to include a contract clause requiring presenters to notify you if they're too ill to speak no more than 48 hours before their talk. This will give you needed time to find a good replacement.

Further, make the simple request to have speakers call or text upon arrival to the hotel. (At No More Boring Meetings, for example, we track each flight and let organizers know the ETA of their out-of-towners, in real time.)

Tip 5 **Manage a speaker no-show**

Despite your best efforts, if you still end up with a speaker no show, here are some creative options for how to manage the situation:

→ Ask a (qualified!) speaker on your agenda to take your no-show speaker's place.

→ See if other organizations are holding meetings in or near your venue on the same dates, and inquire about whether a speaker on their agenda may be a good fit for you.

→ Contact your favorite speakers' bureau. They can search for presenters by region in a flash, have deep relationships with speakers of all types and will act fast to resolve this crisis.

→ Tap into a local college or university for specialized experts. Someone may be just a call or a text away.

And, keep the following in your back pocket as stress-saving "insurance policies:"

→ Select an additional replacement speaker when booking your "planned-for" expert. Contract with this replacement to be "on call" in case of a no-show—either accessible on that day by phone or, better yet, in *person* at the meeting. While this option will probably require a fee, it is likely much less expensive—in dollars and reputation—than no speaker at all.

→ Turn to your leadership for, say, a candid "view-from-the-trenches" Q&A, a panel discussion or a talk show. You'll save the day by increasing the access to executives in the eyes of attendees, *and* boosting the depth of the overall education. (For tips, see Chapter 6: How to Use Panels, Q&A Sessions and Event Hosts.)

→ Plan a relevant activity in lieu of the external speaker's session. This could include a facilitator-led discussion on the original keynote topic or a networking segment, for example. (See Chapter 8: Unconventional Event Formats for more ideas.)

How to Manage the Details for Participants and Stakeholders

To plan for a great experience for your attendees and stakeholders, there are a few best practices you should use for every event.

Tip 1 **Smooth sailing upon arrival**

Ensure that speakers and entertainers have everything at their disposal to arrive at the right venue, at the right time, in the right room. This one's not as obvious as you would think. Give yourself some peace of mind by providing all travelers accurate driving directions, parking information, your full meeting agenda, meeting room name, a building map, and the name and cell phone of the performers' main onsite contact.

Tip 2 **Are you prepared for your VIPs?**

Be sure all your VIPs' and sponsors' needs (as specified in their contracts) are met as promised. I speak from experience when I say that sometimes these promises can fall through the cracks. How you show the love to your "most importants" deeply matters—free parking, reception rooms, signed books, special meals, behind-the-scenes entrances and exits, box seats. Maybe even pair them with a liaison throughout the event for an extra level of care.

Tip 3 **I can't hear you now**

In this era of constant conductivity, it's never been more important for your guests to be able to enjoy a seamless online experience. My event colleagues and I got a hard lesson in this when we tried to stage a cutting-edge augmented reality experience at a live event and underestimated the needed bandwidth, causing the vendor exhibit to be sub-optimized. As a result, the sponsor was understandably disappointed. Grr!

Looking back, we realize we could have tested the level of needed bandwidth by rehearsing the AR experience in an actual crowd, not just basing our set up on the equipment vendor's estimates. Obvious now, but not obvious at the time. So, it belongs here, in the non-obvious event guide!

Tip 4 **I can't see or hear you now**

Make sure that you set up your room optimally for attendees. For many event types, I highly recommend curved theater seating, illustrated here. This set up maximizes sight lines, movement, as well as participants' abilities to see, hear and share insights with one another. This all may seem, um, obvious, but in my experience, many organizers default to straight rows of seats facing front, which stifles interaction and engagement on every level.

Curved theater seating maximizes participants' abilities to see and interact with each other

STAGE/FRONT OF ROOM

TIP: Maintain a tight space between stage & first rows.

Tip 5 **The wisdom of crowds**

You and your team have worked for months to design and now go live with your event. You've planned everything down to the last detail. Except for one. You're thirty minutes from a 9 A.M. show time, and because they are human, hundreds of your guests have arrived almost all at once. While you'd said doors open at 8 A.M.—and had *assumed* many would arrive by then—most have shown up at 8:30, and now you have a massive bottleneck, *and the devil,* at your door. The entire day's schedule will be off, and people will be miffed, right from the start. Bloody _____! Next time, consult with venue representatives and registration experts to develop a proven crowd-control plan specific to your space, so guests stay calm, and you do, too.

Tip 6 **Practice doing things wrong: The pre-mortem**

Most event organizers conduct post-mortems, when it's too late to fix problems. But you can uncover non-obvious problems before they happen by holding a pre-mortem. In this keep-the-devil-at-bay business strategy, you imagine, in great detail, how every element of your event can fail, so you're ready for just about anything. In the process, you'll generate a set of clear action plans, avoid holding a gathering that

is ever in dire need of resuscitating and be prepared
for whatever unfolds. Check out this easy-to-follow
example for some worst-case-scenarios—and how to
mitigate each.

Programming element	What could go wrong	Preventive step(s)
Registration	Website goes down, preventing registration; not enough people for food-and-beverage minimum	Be sure webhost has backup system; have a plan for what F&B you'll add to make up the difference between the contracted minimum and your order
Event sells out	Registration software doesn't support taking a wait list	Get software that does allow for a wait list (such as EventBrite)
Attendee arrival	Attendee lines back up, causing delayed start; Wi-Fi down so can't register people day of; printer breaks/unable to print name tags	Add staff to manage lines; add a solutions desk; get Wi-Fi hotspots; buy blank name badge labels and markers to hand-write nametags in a pinch
Pre-conference session	Too many people to fit in the room and a tussle breaks out	Create a wait-list plan and plant a room monitor to ensure capacity is not exceeded
Break	Food runs out half way through; no coffee available	Triple check minimums with caterer; know where nearest Starbucks is located and pick a runner who can do last-minute pick up

Keynote 1	Speaker no-show; speaker runs over by fifteen minutes	Contract with backup speaker in advance or have a planned-for activity in lieu of speaker; place a large clock on stage and reinforce timeline with all speakers
Break	Attendee chokes on pretzel	Review and practice safety procedures with venue and event team during pre-con meeting (See Chapter 12: How to Plan an Event on (Almost) Any Timeline for details)
Breakout sessions	Miscalculated # of rooms needed; a speaker's computer (containing her deck) crashes just before start	Triple check agenda against room setup requests; ensure that all speakers send their decks in advance and load on your laptops or via the cloud; if the speaker won't send deck in advance, insist that she have it backed up on flash drive
Lunch	Host gets laryngitis	Arrange for internal team member to know and rehearse script; bring stash of honey, lemon, lozenges
Keynote 2	Power goes out; last-minute tech issues for customer story live via Skype; video's audio doesn't work, despite testing	Confirm and review venue's backup power plan; pre-record customer story as a backup; name someone who, in a pinch, could lip-synch the audio (you'll generate laughs and save the day)
Social action activity outside	Unexpected heavy rains mean even the ground under tent is too soggy	Reserve an inside room for activity or arrange backup activity not dependent on outside space

Closing reception	Two people from competing company's sales team show up and try to talk with your top customer	Use a "bouncer" at entry doors who watches for interlopers without name badges

CHAPTER SUMMARY:
THREE THINGS TO REMEMBER

→ Ensure you include everything you need in offers to external speakers; ask presenters to dress in colors that contrast with the staging backdrop so that they're more visible to the audience and on video; in advance, develop a fail-safe plan for mitigating or preventing speaker no-shows.

→ Curved theater seating maximizes audience engagement (see diagram).

→ Stage a pre-mortem so you're ready for just about anything.

CHAPTER 14

How to Take Smart Risks (And Why You Need To)

The events industry tends to view risk as a liability. We have (and need!) complex contractual clauses that address indemnity, force majeure and liability. We use carefully crafted checklists, so events run effectively. After all, who wants to risk it?

Then we invite imperfect, easily bored guests whose attention spans we cannot control. We host folks who crave novelty, surprise, creativity and truly cutting-edge ideas.

As we consider risk on a continuum, I believe there's an inherent—and crucial—boldness in trying something new with our programming design and not knowing, for certain, whether it'll work.

I believe that for us to truly raise the bar on and positively change the overall event experience, *we* need to change. And change doesn't happen in the middle. It happens on the *edge*, where it's *uncomfortable.*

After all, it's when participants are uncomfortable, faced with the unknown and full of curiosity, that change and transformation happen.

Put another way: "Discomfort is a proxy for progress," noted TED's Chris Anderson at TED2018.[19]

So how do we navigate the gap between staging safe, legal, well-run events (Job #1) and producing live experiences that leave audiences changed and inspired (Job #2)?

Let's explore how to find a useful balance between being careful when careful is called for and creative in ways attendees crave.

For the record, I'm not suggesting we re-invent and change up everything about every event. That is unnecessary and impractical. Successful risk taking is incremental risk taking. If it seems more palatable, use the term "experiment" in place of "risk."

 ## Explain the Why of Your Risks

We can begin by communicating to our stakeholders and audiences the why behind our risks.

Attendees want and deserve to know the reasons you're trying something new, and will tolerate more risk if they understand your why. And if you don't have specific reasons for sticking your neck out to launch something new, then do reconsider your choice.

ORION FIRST

Orion First, an industry leader in small business commercial finance, has been holding a regional Lending Forum since 2003. Its initial structure: gather bank partner clients, and in a roundtable format, give them updates on Orion, its accomplishments and its outlook on finance and small-business lending.

Then a few years ago, the team realized this self-serving agenda, essentially all about them and not about the needs of the audience, was—you guessed it!—more boring than ROAR-ing.

They decided to retool, and asked: "How can we add more value from the attendees' point of view?" Ever since, the Forum has become a larger, national conference featuring headlining speakers and thought leaders who deliver relevant and actionable professional development content. There are interactive breakouts and attendee-led panels via which participants openly share ideas, best practices and the challenges of lending.

The event now takes a meatier look into what the future may hold, and collectively helps attendees sharpen their craft.

A much more diverse set of attendees, including those from publicly traded companies, come now not just from the Pacific Northwest, but from all over the country, as the Forum moved from Tacoma, WA, to Denver, CO. Between 2016 and 2017 (when they became a No More Boring Meetings client), attendance grew 20%.

Getting here took substantial risks: taking Orion employees "off the selling floor" for a few days. Asking most attendees, too, to fly in. Securing sponsors to underwrite increased expenses (because the event is offered to registrants at no cost). Not knowing how people would respond to a new format.

The biggest risks? According to CEO David Schaefer, they are: keeping the Lending Forum the same, not growing and becoming irrelevant.

David and his team asked: What's our bigger why? And the answer: We do this work to help fuel the catalytic power of small business, which in turn brings more value back to the communities we and all small businesses serve. To that end, a relationship-building golf tournament as part of the Lending Forum experience directly supports YMCA programs.

How to Successfully Integrate Risk

And another example of a successful event risk:

Imagine trying to set the stage for managers to be more change-ready in a meeting structured the same old way. Talk about a disconnect! A client of mine needed to increase attendee buy-in on new change initiatives in three divisions. I proposed that if we were introducing the concept of change, the structure of the event needed to be changed.

Her verbalized "why" for the event audience might sound like this: "We decided to exemplify what being change-ready looks like by changing up our programming this afternoon. Let's get started with a quiz, a roundtable and a hot seat with execs where we'll get into the trenches of what the future can look like."

First, the participants experienced a "Fact or Crap" game through which everyone was quizzed on their knowledge of the firm's and industry's changes over the years. It was playful, but had a more serious purpose: to open meeting goers' minds to moving through the policy and personnel changes on the horizon.

Starting with a game lessened resistance to what came next in the event agenda, which included announcements about

how participants would
be personally affected by
change initiatives.

Next, the group participated in highly relevant table-top conversations focused on upcoming initiatives that would require them to use their change-management skills. Managers were able to learn from each other and share best practices for problem-solving.

In another segment, leaders sat on stage in "Hot Seats," while attendees submitted anonymous questions. As noted later in the debrief, the rapid-fire Q&A boosted managers' trust in their leaders and served as a fresh way to communicate the challenges and rewards ahead—with a human touch. This all happened without a slide deck getting in the way of having *engaging, inclusive* conversations.

My client's own manager thanked her for raising the bar on their events. Attendees expressed appreciation for the new formats. They knew they covered a great deal of important ground, yet didn't feel rushed—or bored.

Failure *is* an option.

An unavoidable component of risk is failure. Like it or not, we learn more from messing up than getting it right.

Working with a financial services client, I once made the mistake of using too many new formats at the organization's training event. Change is good—but too much of it, all at once, can backfire. My hard lesson is now offered to you so you can steer clear of this misjudgment: Take risks one by one, and achieve small wins over time.

Author Harriet Rubin's advice sustained me as I riskily launched my own entrepreneur-ship in 1999. Her words still inspire me:

"At some point, we all have to decide how we are going to fail: by not going far enough, or by going too far. The only alternative for the most successful (maybe even the most fulfilled) people is the latter. The interesting challenge is to know that if you don't go far enough, you'll never know how far you can go."[20]

GET REAL:

Consider a risk you've taken. Looking back, what was the biggest lesson from it? How does that awareness inform how you'll take a risk on your next event?

 CHAPTER SUMMARY:
THREE THINGS TO REMEMBER

→ To change and improve the overall event experience, we need to change as event managers by experimenting with incremental, thoughtful risks.

→ Start by communicating to stakeholders and audiences the why behind your risks, because attendees want and deserve to know the reasons you're trying something new, and they'll then be more supportive of the risks.

→ One company successfully took a battery of risks to transform their event by asking, "How can we add more value from the attendees' point of view, and make the event content all about them?"

Encore! Encore! Extending Learning and Boosting Value Before and After Events

We ask much of our events, and the people who attend them. We want our participants to learn to manage change. To be inspired to contribute hard-earned money to fight cancer. To be *transformed* into more effective leaders.

All in an event lasting a few hours or a few days.

There's one big problem with these important and valiant goals. They're almost always unrealistic. Mental and behavioral shifts in learning, inspiration and transformation usually take a lot longer than events themselves last. And they require a great deal more than a visit from the likes of Tony Robbins. (You may be surprised to hear this rarely-mentioned truth from the longtime owner of a speakers' bureau, of all people!)

So, let's get real again.

In this chapter, we'll explore tools and tactics that, when implemented, will help you extend the value, impact and applications of your events, so you can stack the deck toward more lasting, positive shifts in performance. This will ensure your attendees will enjoy the very best experience you can muster—before and long after they depart.

We can boost the returns you generate from your tireless effort and substantial investments. And in many cases, do so without spending much more.

We'll give your people a fish—and teach them to fish for themselves.

 ## Pre-Event Engagement Extenders

Even if your attendees know each other, and especially if they don't, it's up to you to help create a sense of belonging and community before they arrive at your event. You then lay the groundwork for deeper trust, networking and cohesion.

Obvious (and still important): Consider creating speaker-produced videos to build program awareness and buzz. Or a closed, attendee-only Facebook or LinkedIn group. Or a tweet-up (an organized, in-person gathering of people on Twitter).

→ **Announce to all your presenters—and tell attendees—that there will be a contest:** Attendees will vote on the best idea presented during a live program, and the winner will receive a (sponsor-provided?) prize. This both raises the bar on the quality of presentations, *and* builds engagement (audiences better pay attention!). Also consider giving contributors who vote a special prize or an early-bird discount to your next event. This encourages and rewards future attendance.

→ **Organize attendee-only meet ups** in cities from which your registrants hail. These can be as simple as happy hours, or you could offer a framework for something like regional book clubs.

→ Producing an event with out-of-town guests? **Set up a (sponsor-supported?) registration and event check-in lounge at the main airport.** We all know first impressions matter, and this pre-event engagement extender will go a long way in helping attendees feel immediately welcomed, boosting networking and creating a sense of belonging right from the get go.

→ **Gather event registrants together to watch a TED Talk,** choosing a talk by a speaker who's present-

ing at your event. (Check TED's licensing rules in
advance and be sure the content in the video footage is distinct from what the speaker will present
live.)

→ Global TED event delegates are encouraged to
bring one gift to share with another participant.
TED then matches people up. Because these event
audiences are global, a gift from a home city works
well. At TEDSummit, a global TED event for innovators and entrepreneurs, I exchanged gifts with
a man from Tokyo. He gave me wooden TEDxTo-
kyo-branded sake glasses, and was over the moon
about the Rain Globe gift I gave. (It's a snow globe
that rains. I hail from soggy Seattle, after all!) The
only cost for event organizers: a bit of setup time.
After that, *participants* give it life, often sharing it
on social media to amplify its impact.

 15.2 ## Post-Event Engagement Extenders

Your *fête* appears to be finished because everyone's
gone home.

Ah, but not so fast. Let's explore ways to extend the life,
vibe and takeaways of your meeting long after the last
ovation.

An organization called Liberating Structures has developed a construct that's useful to us in this context, because it urges us to intentionally shape the future. It's called "What, So What, Now What?" Or W^3.[21]

Accordingly, we ask: **What** happened? **So what** if it did? **Now what** do we do about it? This simple formula helps us leverage our content and intentionally build a framework for further exploration.

And as we discussed in Chapter 2: How We Learn, we only learn new ideas after repeated exposure to them. So, if you're not reinforcing the most important takeaways from your event in your follow-up, then you may as well have not offered them in the first place.

 ## "What, So What, Now What?"

What happened? What did you see? What stood out?

So What? Why is that important? What patterns, actions and conclusions emerge?

Now What? What follow-up actions make sense? What takeaways can we activate for application in the real world?

Obvious: Webinars. Learning management systems offered by many speakers as value-add educational tools. Google Hangouts.

NON-OBVIOUS:

→ **A Post-Program Pair-Up** is a simple, powerful exercise I've designed to increase networking and the likelihood of positive change. Whether you have 50 or 5,000 attendees, near the end of your event, have your host pair up participants. Ask each person in these dyads to discuss one new goal they want to reach in the next thirty days. They then record their objectives—plus each other's contact information—and together commit to reaching these milestones. Smaller audience? Take commitments to a higher level: Invite everyone to state their goals before the whole group, as sharing a goal publicly means that you're more likely to succeed.

→ **Second Loop of Learning**: When working with corporate teams, speaker Dr. John Izzo takes the Post-Program Pair-Up a step further. In his model, both event goers *and* organizational leadership commit to what they're going to achieve after the event. Leaders send an email to attendees about how they will apply what they learned and by what date. In this ongoing loop, leaders report back on their own progress and challenges, and ask audience members for input on how they're doing in reaching their goals. Results: deeper engagement, leadership transparency and more goals realized. (In lieu of email, everyone can post to a private social media page, if you prefer.)

→ **Launch a Wiki, Basecamp or proprietary platform** on which participants may share and mine ideas, videos, white papers and case studies that reveal how ideas from your event are being activated in the real world. For little or no investment, this collective, user-generated content can last well beyond an event's timeline, drastically increase its takeaway value and boost return attendance. Expand it further by securing a sponsor whose mission aligns with yours.

→ **The Gift that Keeps on Giving:** Find a sponsor (tips for doing so are in Chapter 7: How to Maximize Your Budget) with an exclusive product aligned to your event, and have the company send one to every attendee. According to Event Marketer, 74% of attendees feel more positively about a brand or product that's promoted after they've attended an event.[22]

Non-Obvious Tools to Enhance the Attendee Experience

The term "attendee experience" refers to every aspect of how guests take in a gathering: from the very first moment they visit an event website, to long after the

event ends. So, what can you do—beyond the obvious—
to make your conference more memorable and
seamless?

→ **Conduct a communication audit** to ensure all
event messaging speaks to the needs and motives
of attendees—not to those of your organization.

→ **Provide extra care for early arrivals** by hosting
a social event for people who come in before the
main event begins, so they immediately feel a part
of the event "tribe."

→ How can you add fun and functionality to name
badges, as well as easily create subgroups that
share certain interests? **Try an "Ask me about"
line**. At registration, have people share, say, three
words that summarize their personal or professional interests. And print those words on each
name badge to make it easy for strangers to
converse. For example, my TEDActive badge read,
"meeting engagement – unplugging – cocktails."

→ If some event content focuses on sensitive issues,
establish a room where folks can decompress
and even talk to someone about thoughts and
feelings the program triggered.

→ **Run through the entire event** a week or two
ahead as if you were an attendee—looking for
problem areas and sources of discomfort.

→ If applicable, **tell your live audience about any future events** you're hosting to help generate buzz. Can you even register people on site for upcoming gatherings while they're in the midst of your positive event experience?

→ Once the event concludes, how will you communicate and engage with guests in ways that **extend the event experience**? Post-event summary videos? A book club? A monthly newsletter? Contests for applying what they learned? Niche clubs that meet outside your larger event?

15.5 Openers, Closers and "Bookends"

Start and end your meeting by reinforcing your theme, goals and key messages. My clients add elements such as skits, retrospective videos, talk shows, custom songs, graphic illustration and games that reinforce main points and tie metaphorical and memorable "ribbons" around programming.

Or you may want to "bookend" content. This means staging a memorable, high-energy, messaged-aligned opening that dovetails effectively with your closing. Some ideas include:

→ **Invite a local high school marching band** (read: no cost) to energetically lead your audience, *en masse,* into the ballroom to open the event. At the end, your audience—now deeply connected as a team, as a tribe—*becomes a band.* You've given them all drums and/or other instruments, and with your host-turned-conductor's guidance, they generate an easy, powerful rhythm themselves as they move out of the venue. Simple, low-cost, high-energy, inclusive and fun.

→ Or **start your meeting with a keynote** in which you announce a new company initiative. End with an all-voices heard, customized company anthem, featuring how this initiative will be executed—which sends everyone off on the highest possible note.

→ A recent client wanted to **integrate a "whodunnit" game** into their annual all-hands meeting. Like any good mystery, the game had employees on a search for the "victims" and "perpetrators." Knowing that the main purpose of the gathering had a more serious purpose of helping employees manage change more effectively, I made the connection between the fun of the game, and the very significant downside of employees who do not manage change well. They tend to think of themselves as *victims*, and the company as the *perpetrator.* So, we set the stage for them becoming better change managers by asking as the event ended: will you be the *victim, or the victor?* What role might *you* play in perpetrating an old, outdated way of looking at an ever-evolving world?

Whether an hour, a day or a week in length, your event—when "bookended"—will be more memorable, Tweetable and rave-worthy.

 ## GET REAL:

Speaking of closers and bookends, here we are at the end of our time together. This is the ideal moment to "Get Real" once more and bring together the strategies, tools and insights we've covered.

To that end, answer for yourself the "What, So What, Now What?" (W^3) questions by plugging in your event variables so that you can effectively design and execute an encore-worthy experience at your next shindig.

Until we meet again...

I'm grateful for your company on this learning journey. Now, let's go inspire the masses with our collective kick-assery!

Please email questions, comments and stories related to what this guide inspires you to produce via Engage@NoMoreBoringMeetings.com.

CHAPTER SUMMARY:
THREE THINGS TO REMEMBER

→ Extend value and impact via non-obvious pre-event engagement extenders, such as a check-in lounge at the nearest airport or a connection-rich gift exchange among attendees...and post-event engagement extenders such as the Post-Program Pair-Up.

→ Use the "What, So What, Now What?" construct to leverage meeting content and build a framework for future exploration.

→ Stage a memorable, viral-worthy close by turning your attendee base into a massive marching band, or sing a custom anthem as everyone departs.

Acknowledgments (AKA gratitudes, not platitudes!)

Just before beginning to write this book, I learned a wonderful, new word: ecstasis. It's the "act of stepping beyond oneself," in a way that catalyzes a powerful connection to a greater intelligence; to a state of possibility, awareness and activation. I refer to this delicious word in the body of the book, because to me it's the ultimate goal—and a most powerful outcome—of a kick-ass event.

Ecstasis deserves a bit more ink again here in these acknowledgments, as it also beautifully illustrates how so many people stepped up to provide me with a "greater intelligence" that's helped make this guide possible.

TRUSTED ADVISORS:

I raise my glass to these smarty pants, who in their own distinct, wise ways provided valued perspectives, expertise and support: Shawn Achor, Holli Catchpole, Elizabeth Coppinger, Curtis Costner, Lisa Phelps

Dawes, Lori Dennis, Debra Fine, Meredith Lee, Angee Linsey, Amy Lynch, David Schaefer, Bill Stainton, Jane Tornatore and Mark Turner.

CHEERLEADERS:

Move aside, NFL cheerleading squads. A stadium's worth of pom-pom waving goes to these fine humans who supported me throughout. First, a special thanks to Jane Driessen. She flew a vibrant flag of encouragement with the same fervor I think our late father and mother, Leo and Fran, would have; their influences live on in these pages.

Deep gratitude as well to Sara Abel, Posy Gering, Jill Hashimoto, Saskia Houwing, Alison Kartiganer, Kate Kotecki, Valerie Rivera, Amy Sanders, Bill Schultheis and Lorie Thomas.

Plus, a special shout out to Michael Pinchera, who's been instrumental in my journey as a published author.

BOOK TEAM:

Publisher Rohit Bhargava, for offering the opportunity to write this guide in the first place! Editor Gretchen Gardner, for bringing a finely tuned macro-micro zoom lens capable of both big-picture insights and in-the-trenches tweaks; her smarts and vigilance have made this guide oh-so-much better. Renee Strom for her generous introductions. And production maven Marnie McMahon for deftly managing everything else.

YOU:

Thank you for reading. If you found it valuable, tell Amazon. If you didn't, tell me!

The Non-Obvious Further Reading List

Best Things I've Ever Read

The Attention Economy: Understanding the New Currency of Business, by Thomas H. Davenport and John C. Beck

Big Potential, by Shawn Achor

Brain Rules: 12 Principles for Surviving and Thriving at Work, Home and School, by Dr. John Medina

Can You Hear Me? How to Connect with People in a Virtual World, by Nick Morgan

The Experience Economy, by B. Joseph Pine II and James H. Gilmore

Focus: The Hidden Driver of Excellence, by Daniel Goleman

Gamestorming: A Playbook for Innovators, Rulebreakers, and Changemakers, by Dave Gray, Sunni Brown, and James Macanufo

Impro, by Keith Johnstone

Make It Stick: The Science of Successful Learning, by Peter C. Brown, Henry L. Roediger III, and Mark A. McDaniel

The Paradox of Choice: Why More Is Less, by Barry Schwartz

The Power of Participation, by Adrian Segar

Powerful Panels: A Step-by-Step Guide to Moderating Lively & Informative Panel Discussions at Meetings, Conferences & Conventions, by Kristin Arnold

Presentation Zen: Simple Ideas on Presentation Design and Delivery, by Garr Reynolds

Resonate: Present Visual Stories that Transform Audiences, by Nancy Duarte

Sensation: The New Science of Physical Intelligence, by Thalma Lobel

SPARK: The Revolutionary New Science of Exercise and the Brain, by John J. Ratey, MD

Stealing Fire, by Steven Kotler and Jamie Wheal

TED Talks, by Chris Anderson

Total Engagement: How Games and Virtual Worlds Are Changing the Way People Work and Businesses Compete, by Byron Reeves and J. Leighton Read

Kick-Ass Online Resources

The Club at No More Boring Meetings

http://www.nomoreboringmeetings.com/club

No More Boring Meetings' video resources

https://www.youtube.com/nomoreboringmeetings

No More Boring Meetings Blog

http://www.nomoreboringmeetings.com/blog/

Nick Morgan, Public Words

http://www.publicwords.com/blog/

Velvet Chainsaw (content, conference and trade show strategy firm)

https://velvetchainsaw.com/

Compelling Conferences to Check Out

Aspen Ideas Festival
https://www.aspenideas.org/, a gathering for cross-discipline leaders who engage in deep and inquisitive discussion of a wide range of issues

Convening Leaders
http://conveningleaders.org/, Professional Convention Management Association's annual conference

EG
https://www.egconf.com/, founded by Richard Saul Wurman, who also founded TED & TEDMED conferences

The FRESH Conference
https://www.thefreshconference.com, a global hybrid event focused on the latest in meeting design

Great Ideas Conference
https://www.greatideasconference.org, American Society of Association Executives' flagship innovation conference for association leaders from around the world

PopTech
http://poptech.org/, which convenes a community of scientists, technologists, humanitarians, designers, artists, innovators, corporate and governmental leaders and academics to push the limits of possibility

World Education Congress
https://www.mpiweb.org/events, Meeting Professionals International's annual conference

Endnotes

Chapter 2: How We Learn: Why Some Events Work Better Than Others

1. **Why learning only happens with time and reflection. Author interview with Jeff Hurt of Velvet Chainsaw, 2018.** https://velvetchainsaw.com.

2. **How to boost memory and recall. From the book** *Brain Rules: 12 Principles for Surviving and Thriving at Work, Home and School* (updated and expanded edition), by Dr. John Medina, www.BrainRules.net.

Chapter 3: How to Transform Attendees into Participants

3. **How to exercise boosts brain power. From the book** *Brain Rules: 12 Principles for Surviving and Thriving at Work, Home and School* (updated and expanded edition), by Dr. John Medina, www.BrainRules.net and www.brainrules.net/references.

4. **The influence of exercise on cognitive abilities. Scientific studies based on neuroimaging show how physical activity improves cognition. Read the study:** https://onlinelibrary.wiley.com/doi/full/10.1002/cphy.c110063.

5. **Why exercise improves learning. From Dr. John Ratey's TEDxManhattanBeach talk. More background can be found in his book,** *SPARK: The Revolutionary New Science of Exercise and the Brain.*

6. **How to structure event programming to maintain optimal brain function. From the book** *Before Happiness: The 5 Hidden Keys to Achieving Success, Spreading Happiness, and Sustaining Positive Change,*

by Shawn Achor. And from https://www.nytimes.com/2011/08/21/magazine/do-you-suffer-from-decision-fatigue.html that reports on research showing how our most important decisions should not happen in the hour before a meal, in a study showing how judges' decisions on granting parole vary widely when correlated with when they eat.

7. **The power of *ecstasis*, the "act of stepping beyond oneself." From the book** *Stealing Fire: How Silicon Valley, the Navy Seals, and Maverick Scientists are Revolutionizing the Way we Live and Work,* by Steven Kotler and Jamie Wheal.

8. **The best foods for the learning brain. From article by wellness expert Jennifer Cohen, 12 Best Foods To Boost Brain Power. Read it here:** https://www.forbes.com/sites/jennifercohen/2015/02/05/12-best-foods-to-boost-brain-power/2/#53da773556d3.

Chapter 4: Why You Need More Engagement and How to Get It

9. **Generational differences in how people prefer to learn. Author interview with generational consultant Amy Lynch,** www.generationaledge.com.

10. **The effects of music on brainwaves. From the book** *Stealing Fire: How Silicon Valley, the Navy Seals, and Maverick Scientists are Revolutionizing the Way we Live and Work,* by Steven Kotler and Jamie Wheal.

11. **Our 10-minute attention spans and the importance of repeating information to remember and recall it. From the book** *Brain Rules: 12 Principles for Surviving and Thriving at Work, Home and School* (updated and expanded edition), by Dr. John Medina, www.BrainRules.net and www.brainrules.net/references.

12. **Keeping a meeting room on one level to build consensus. From** *Sensation: The New Science of Physical Intelligence,* by Thalma Lobel, www.thalmalobel.com.

13. **Engaging attendees in virtual and hybrid events. Author interview with Glenn Thayer,** www.emcee.com.

Chapter 5: How to Curate a Kick-Ass Speaker Lineup

14. **Don't assume speakers capable of delivering a TED or TEDx talk are equally adept at delivering a full-length keynote. Article by speaker bureau veteran Brian Palmer, in the** *Meeting Professional Magazine***, July 2016.**

Chapter 8: Unconventional Event Formats That Boost Engagement

15. **Rich mix of fresh event formats.** Author interview with Jim Gilmore, 2018.

Chapter 9: How to Effectively Use Humor and Infotainment

16. **Use of humor in hospice and palliative care industry.** Author interview with Barbara Bouton of National Hospice and Palliative Care Organization, 2018.

Chapter 10: How to Think Like a TED Conference Organizer

17. **Worthy TED Talk topics are dreams bigger than we are that become ideas we rebuild in the minds of listeners. From the book** *TED Talks*, by Chris Anderson, head of TED.

Chapter 11: How to Produce and Stage Manage an Event Like a Pro

18. **The differences in brain activity between active and passive learners, and how activity enhances learning. In the journal** *Nature Neuroscience* **as reported by the University of Illinois news bureau:** https://news.illinois.edu/view/6367/205467.

Chapter 14: How to Take Smart Risks (And Why You Need To)

19. **"Discomfort is a proxy for progress." Overheard by author at TED2018.**

20. **"At some point, we all have to decide how we are going to fail...." Quote by Harriet Rubin in her book,** *Soloing: Realizing Your Life's Ambition.*

Chapter 15: Encore! Encore! Extending Learning and Boosting Value Before and After Events

21. **What, So What, Now What? Or W³ concept. Developed by Liberating Structures:** www.liberatingstructures.com.

22. **74% of attendees feel more positively about a brand or product that's promoted after they've attended an event. Based on a study by the Event Marketing Institute and the experiential agency Mosaic, which sponsor an annual survey called EventTrack. Read about the study:** http://blog.pop2life.com/blog/18-experiential-marketing-stats-for-2018.

Author Biography

Andrea Driessen, Chief Boredom Buster at Seattle, WA-based No More Boring Meetings, is an internationally award-winning business owner who stages engaging, unconventional events with compelling thought leaders, fresh meeting formats and purposeful play. Her clients' gatherings have participants returning to work ready to perform at their very best. A Professional Convention Management Association "Best-in-Class" speaker and thirty-year event-industry veteran, Andrea has helped organize TEDxSeattle for seven years, and is a TEDSummit and TEDActive attendee.

Index